Arthur Brinkman

The Controversial Methods of Romanism

Arthur Brinkman

The Controversial Methods of Romanism

ISBN/EAN: 9783744664479

Printed in Europe, USA, Canada, Australia, Japan

Cover: Foto ©Thomas Meinert / pixelio.de

More available books at **www.hansebooks.com**

THE METAPHYSICS OF JOHN STUART MILL.

BY

W. L. COURTNEY, M.A.,

FELLOW OF NEW COLLEGE, OXFORD.

LONDON:
C. KEGAN PAUL & CO., 1, PATERNOSTER SQUARE.
1879.

[The rights of translation and of reproduction are reserved.]

PREFACE.

THIS book is an attempt to deal in somewhat cursory fashion with large metaphysical problems. Questions of Philosophy almost necessarily involve an abstruse mode of treatment, intricate details, and a technical phraseology, which make them difficult and repellent to the majority of the reading public; while the attempt to treat them in a simple and broad manner, without the use of a peculiar nomenclature, seems fore-doomed to ignore their complexity and arduousness. Whether it is possible to steer clear of either misfortune is, perhaps, doubtful: all that I have tried to do in the following pages is to avoid prolixity, and to set as clearly as I could before the reader the main issue between rival systems. Originality I cannot and do not claim.

That Mr. Mill's logical and psychological speculations distinctly raise metaphysical questions is in itself a proof of the reality of Metaphysics. Every system must of necessity rest on the basis of some theory of "Consciousness," and "Consciousness" brings inevitably in its train metaphysical problems. Even a physiologist like Mr. George Henry Lewes finds, in his "Problems of Life and Mind," that the Positive Philosophy must seek to lay, as best it can, the Metaphysical ghost, which is ever starting up with awkward persistence to confront experimental psychology and demonstrated materialism.

It only remains for me to acknowledge assistance received from one or two friends, especially Mr. F. H. Bradley, Fellow of Merton College, Oxford. Most of all, however, I am indebted to Professor Green's Introduction to the Philosophy of Hume,—a work to which many of these pages owe any value they may contain.

OXFORD, *November*, 1878.

CONTENTS.

		PAGE
CHAP.	I.—INTRODUCTORY	1
,,	II.—THE ANTECEDENTS OF MILL. HUME	16
,,	III.—THE ANTECEDENTS OF MILL (*continued*)	27
,,	IV.—CONSCIOUSNESS	44
,,	V.—BODY AND MIND	63
,,	VI.—THE PRIMARY QUALITIES OF MATTER	81
,,	VII.—CAUSATION, AND THE UNIFORMITY OF NATURE	98
,,	VIII.—MATHEMATICAL AXIOMS AND NECESSARY TRUTHS	116
,,	IX.—GENERAL IDEAS	134
,,	X.—EPILOGUE	148

THE METAPHYSICS

OF

JOHN STUART MILL.

CHAPTER I.

INTRODUCTORY.

THE future of metaphysical speculation is the question which is more and more agitating the modern philosophic mind. Is it doomed to yield to the conquering inroads of "Science," is it, in Mr. Lewes' language "to be crushed into dust beneath the chariot wheels of modern thought?" Or is there yet a region into which Science has never come, into which it cannot come, because Scientific methods cannot be applied to the source and fountain-head of all method whatsoever? Such a question can only be approached when it has become clear with what sort of problems metaphysics deals: it cannot be summarily despatched by the assertion that every such problem, when "rationally stated," is capable of solution by "the inductions and deductions from experience."

The contention of the opponents of metaphysics is that it is totally unprogressive. Here again the whole question turns upon the nature of the progress to be demanded, the character of those landmarks by which advance, retrogression, and lateral oscillation are severally to be estimated. Especially in the judgment to be passed upon a particular philosophical writer, like John Stuart Mill, is it necessary to begin with a preliminary view of intellectual movements in the higher questions of philosophy, if we are in any way to determine the position he is to occupy, and the value to be attributed to his labours. And it is only possible adequately to do this, after a general survey of the lines on which Modern Philosophy has moved for two centuries from Descartes to Hegel.

The period, commencing in the sixteenth century and ending in the eighteenth, exhibits three great movements. At the outset there is the vast dogmatic system of Scholasticism. At the close there is another dogmatic system, rising into prominence, a dogmatism which attempts to construct an ontology out of thought, the system of Hegel. And midway between the two,—in the interspace between the two dogmatisms,—there is a period wherein thought in its newly-found emancipation is running riot in different lines, touching the problems on every side, enquiring critical, tentative, everything but dogmatic, going a few steps in one direction, and then, dissatisfied, turning back on its footsteps and essaying another path, building up only to destroy—a great transitional period, paving the way for a great constructive epoch in the future.

Is there any one description which will suit this period? is there any one aspect which will embrace its various movements? Perhaps only this: a determined assertion of the rights of the individual as against all authority. Authoritative assertion it will have none of: whether it be the authority of the Church, or the authority of Thought in its universal relations, or the authority of a great Matter outside which forces knowledge into conformity with itself. If ever any of these assertions of Authority are made, in however tentative a form, they are immediately destroyed. Scholasticism made the assertion of the Church's Authority: and Bacon and Descartes threw it off. Locke tended to assert the Authority of Matter, and Berkeley threw it off. Berkeley tended to assert the Authority of Spirit or Universal Thought, and Hume threw it off. The right of the individual to construct his own world of Knowledge and Thought and Life,—this is perhaps the one dominant feature of the whole period.

When, after such a general prospect, we look closer into these systems, the action and reaction, the construction and the destruction, the synthesis and the analysis strike us more clearly. Philosophy means Invention, says Bacon: Philosophy means the assertion of myself as a thinking subject, says Descartes. Then follow Materialism in Hobbes, Pantheism in Spinoza, Sensationalism in Locke, Idealism in Berkeley, Scepticism in Hume, Monadism or Individualistic Idealism in Leibnitz, endless analysis in Wolff. The mere terms of description are so antagonistic that the whole period looks like chaos. But this makes still clearer the business of the historian, to disentangle the permanent elements from the transitory, to discover the progressive tendencies, and dissever them from the retrogressive, to let the various systems fall into their proper places of superiority and subordination, to discover which for us are the most important and which most helpful to Thought and Philosophy viewed as a Progress, and not as a chaos of conflicting opinions.

There are two points which are chiefly interesting in studying any period. The first is to see *the limitations of Thought*—to see how Thought, as expressed in the various systems, is limited to one issue rather than another, to the one-sided affirmation of one tendency and the undue depreciation of another tendency. And the second is to see *the Development of Thought*— to deny which is indeed the deathblow of Philosophy, the end of all fruitful relation between Philosophy and Life.

Let us look at the first of these.

Thought, we say, is limited in its expression in any one system. Limited by what? By three things—by the particular character of the knowledge around it, by nationality, by the particular moment at which the system is born.

In Bacon, for instance, there is the enormous and rapid development of physical research going on around him: there is "the moment" wherein the individual thinker was casting off the restraints of authority, whether of Church or of Aristotle: and as to the problem which he assigned to Philosophy, the problem of Invention, or Human Mastery over Nature's secrets,—who can doubt that such a problem essentially suited the character of a grave, practical, active people like the English, with their spirit of enterprise as exhibited in travel, and their intolerance for metaphysics and word-splitting? These, in the sphere of literature, we call "predisposing causes," because in literature the diversity and partiality are recognised elements; but we call them "limitations" in the case of Thought, limitations of that pure, distinctionless spirit, the inmost nature of which must be to be above party or creed or nation.

Or if, leaving Bacon, we look at the course of philosophy as it expressed itself in Locke, and was then extended by Berkeley and Hume, similar results are obtained. We see in Locke the incarnation of the

English philosophic temper, the massive common-sense, the semi-materialism, the practical way of "sending a man back to his senses." But after Locke, tendencies a little alien to the English mind come in,—Berkeley, the too vivacious and spiritual Irishman, attempting to prove that Locke's philosophy led to Idealism, and Hume, the too logical and hard-headed Scotchman, shocking English respectability, by showing that Locke led straight to Scepticism.

I have taken the British philosophers, because it is more easy for us to see in their case these limitations in the expression of Thought; but the same thing would of course be true, among others, of Spinoza and Wolff. Spinoza, the Jew, filled full with the Jewish idea of God's unity and omnipotence, naturally turned his thought into a system of Pantheism; and Wolff, the German, with his patient analysis, with his spider-like propensity of evolving thought out of himself, with his method, his completeness, his dulness—are not these characteristics of *his* nationality?

All these considerations add, I think, to the freshness of interest in studying the History of Philosophy, but they might lead us to serious error. The effect is to make one believe too much in individualities and too little in Thought. Philosophy is too sacred and too impersonal a thing to be resolved into mere conditions and limitations of epochs or nationalities or individual tempers. Let us then try to correct this

INTRODUCTORY.

by turning to the other point of interest, the Development of Thought. In the vast and multiform movement of thought during the seventeenth and eighteenth centuries, what elements of permanent acquisition in Philosophy were being brought to light? What threads may we disentangle from the complex web to give the clue to the new pattern?

The first I will instance is the meaning and proper content of the word " Individual." That looks an insignificant result assuredly. But it is not so really; it carries with it far weightier consequences than would appear at first sight. What, in the first place, is an Individual object? We apprehend many such every day of our lives, and without analysis we should say that an individual object of perception was the effect or result of a single unrelated moment of consciousness, taking in or grasping a single unrelated thing. That is, in truth, the way it strikes Locke; he is, as a philosopher, exactly in the same position as we are in our unanalytic common-sense moods. But then it is from these objects, successively apprehended, that our whole body of knowledge, in some way, grows; and again it is of these objects, single and unrelated, that in some way the world, as a whole, is composed. Now, if we put a number of leaden bullets together, they certainly do not mass themselves into one large leaden bullet by themselves. That is only possible if they are fused together by melting. And a number of single, unrelated objects will never form an articulated world, or a complex body of knowledge, unless they too are in some way fused together. How are they to be fused? The obvious reply is, that the mind invents some links or relations between them. Are these links, then, formed by the mind, purely fictitious, mere inventions? Yes, answer Locke and Hume, they are not found in the constitution of things. Then the world, as a totality, and not as a mere heap of objects, is a delusion? Yes. And knowledge, as a synthesis, and as a unity, and not as a succession of single modes of consciousness, is a delusion also? Yes. Here then we have the complete scepticism of Hume. But Philosophy and Knowledge refuse to commit suicide in this way. And so, as the whole conclusion seems to come from the way in which the individual was regarded, Philosophy looks at this "individual" again, to see if it can be defined differently. There are three words : particular, individual, universal, which seem to come in a definite order. Of these, it is "particular" which should properly be applied to the single, unrelated impression, just as it is "universal," which is obviously applied to the synthesis of objects in a world, or a synthesis of perception in knowledge. What then is individual? It is the meeting-point of particular and universal. In an individual object, how much, if we carefully analyse, is involved? This much,—there is

INTRODUCTORY.

the particular impression on the sentient organs, and there is the action of the mind, which grasps this impression, and retains it, by relating it to other impressions: and so the object becomes definite and individual, distinguished from everything else, and yet related to everything else. Another result, too, follows. If the universal element, *i.e.*, the superinduction of relations, really makes a world, and not a mere heap of unrelated objects, it must be due to Thought, that we get a real world at all; or, in other words, Reality is the work of Thought, to be found in thought, and not in a supposed Matter, still less in a series of sensations.

Let us, before leaving this word, "universal," look at it in another way. Take an individual man, a finite individual. Is there such a creature? Spinoza says, No. He is only an unreal fraction of the Universal. Hume would say Yes, the universal, on the contrary, being a mere fiction of the finite individual. Here are the two extremes, and here is the difficulty. An individual man is finite and separate, on the one hand, and yet on the other he can arrive at universal notions and have an idea of Universality whether exhibited in a Perfect God, or a Cosmic Unity. How is this possible? Only, as it seems, in one way: The individual is a junction of the Universal and the Particular, limited as being "a part of this partial world" *—of

* Green's "Hume," p. 131.

matter, as we roughly call it; but transcending his limitations, as being self-conscious,—because Thought is universal.

Such are the momentous issues of a proper appreciation of this word, so simple as it seems,—" Individual."

Again, we can trace the same progress in the proper understanding of such words as Sensation, Perception, Thought. Sensation and Perception are treated as identical, not distinguished, both by Locke and Hume: we cannot say exactly the same of Berkeley, because he seemed to recognise in the second edition of his " Principles," that he would have to distinguish his " idea," or passive sensation, from an active something, which he called " notion."

In reality it appears that Sensation, Perception, and Thought are the correlates of the words, Particular, Individual, Universal. We do not apprehend an Individual by Sensation, as Locke thought. All we can be aware of by Sensation is a single moment of sentience—a momentary modification of our sensibility, which is what we call " Particular." An individual object, however, is *perceived:* a perception, in other words, is the superinduction on the particular element of sensation, of the universal element of Thought-relations. To constitute an individual object, the momentary sensation has to be arrested, fixed, made definite, crystallized, by

INTRODUCTORY.

the putting on of relations, which serve to distinguish it from, and relate it to, everything else. This is Perception—the fusion, as it were, of the universal element of Thought and the particular elements of Sensation.

The inquiry naturally comes after all this,—is not this mere elaborate word-splitting? Does it, after all, make much difference what particular meaning we assign to words of this sort? It makes no difference, it may at once be admitted, to the practical, commonsense man, who wishes to carve out his fortune in his own practical way—any more than it makes any difference to the Scientific man, who wipes away all these mental cobwebs, and applies himself to experiment and the acquisition of knowledge of Nature. The only thing to be remembered is, that underlying all these experiments and all this practical acquaintance with the world, there is the further question, which some minds are compelled to ask, How is Nature, —How is the world, known at all? And then the result comes out, that, despite all this seemingly immediate perception of Nature and the world, the underlying fact is " consciousness," and the apparently external thing is found by an inexorable logic, to be after all a mode of consciousness. Something of course there is of external, something which is, as it were, given to the mind and not manufactured by the mind, but the whole envisagement of the thing, the whole 'entourage,' as it were, which makes it for us a thing at all, is the creation of consciousness.

All this preliminary consideration, the whole of these fundamental conditions, may be taken for granted, but cannot be denied. And the interest for the metaphysical philosopher is just this preliminary consideration, these fundamental conditions, the satisfactory explanation of which means for him progress, and their systematic neglect, or confused treatment, means for him the demolition of all *raison d'être* whatsoever.

And so all these strands of inquiry and speculation, some of which we have been considering, are reduced at length to the one great decisive problem—What is the relation of the Self to the Not-Self, of the Ego to the Non-Ego? To deny the Self, means scepticism and despair of knowledge as a reasoned system, as it did with Hume. To deny the Not-Self, means endless analysis and sterile revolution of thought upon itself, as it did with Wolff. Progressive advance of knowledge, and knowledge as a reasoned system, alike imperatively demand the acknowledgment of both factors, and some necessary relation between the two. What, then, is the relation?

All the speculation of the seventeenth and eighteenth centuries seems to tend to one result, which may thus be summed. The Not-Self is the manifold, the unformed, the ἄπειρον, as it successively comes in upon our sentient organs. A sensation is this momentary stirring of the sensory organs : a Perception is the individualising, the making-definite of the manifold of sensation by the relations imposed by Thought. Thought is two-fold : in relation to Perception, it is the superinduction of forms, of categories : in relation to itself, it is the universal, which *makes* these forms, these categories, the creator of a Real World, as a totality or synthesis of Phenomena, the creator of Knowledge, as a synthesis or totality of Perception, a perfect and complete Self-Consciousness— limited, indeed, in the case of men, by their being finite parts of this finite order, while in God, it is just this Divine Self-Consciousness, apart from and above all such limitations.

Not-Self, Self, God—τὸ ἄπειρον, τὸ πεπερασμένον, τὸ πέρας : these are the successive moments of Metaphysics, and it is in progress to and in realisation of these, that it finds its scope, its justification, and its life.

What the position of Mill is, with regard to this vast intellectual movement, we have now to attempt to discover. For the present, we may just indicate the conditions under which his philosophy is attempted. He is a Sensationalist,—that is, he belongs to that line of English philosophy which commenced with

Hobbes, was continued by Locke and Berkeley, and culminated in Hume. But, if our review of the period be at all correct, Hume represented the high-water mark of this sort of speculation. Therefore Mill must combine with Hume some newer elements. Above all, living in a great scientific age, he must make his peace with Science, which Hume, to say the least, somewhat gravely affronted. And Science, for most thinkers, has only one metaphysical foundation, viz., that of Realism. Therefore Mill has in some way to combine Sensationalism and Realism. He is a Sensationalist in his " Examination of Sir W. Hamilton," and a Realist in his " Logic."

Or let us look at him from a different aspect. He is an Empiricist,—one link in that chain of empirical research which was formulated in the eighteenth century and vastly developed in the nineteenth. But empiricism in the hands of Locke and Hume is individualistic; empiricism in the hands of Herbert Spencer and George Henry Lewes is universalistic. To which of the two species of empiricism does Mill belong? Curiously enough, the "experience" which plays so large a part in his philosophy, belongs to the age which preceded him, not to that of his contemporaries. In other words, not in an age of individualism, he founds his philosophy on the experience of the individual, like Hume, not on that of the race, like Herbert Spencer. Living in the nineteenth century, in the age when conceptions like "evolution" and "development of the race" are in the air, he still turns back to the time when "the historic sense" was hardly born.

CHAPTER II.

THE ANTECEDENTS OF MILL. HUME.

THE spiritual progenitor of Mill is undoubtedly Hume. Without Hume, Mill would not have been possible, just as without Locke and Berkeley, Hume would not have been possible. Yet the relation of Mill and his predecessor is by no means the same as that of Hume and his predecessors. There are times when thought enters—almost without warning—upon a brilliant and rapidly-developing course, when every step forward presents a clearly-defined and continuous progress, " churning life out of a dead level of habit and custom," striking out glints and gleams of meteoric brilliance, till the whole intellectual horizon is glowing with their fires. Such was the brief life of drama in England, or the sudden glory of Athenian art: such too, with more sombre and subdued radiance, was the development of Sensationalism in England from Locke to Hume. In these times, the lineal successor is also the more perfect mouthpiece of the thought; each step brings out the system into sharper and bolder relief.

But in other times, when the animating impulse has subsided, and the Spirit has spent its force, lineal succession becomes mere repetition with variations, dying away into hollower, artificial, capricious echoes. And then the thinker who takes up the mantle that has dropped from his predecessor's shoulders, is merely sewing pieces of new cloth into the old raiment, whereby the rents are made worse.

The peculiar merit of Hume, as a philosopher, consists in his superior consistency. With him, the doctrines of Sensationalism which he inherited, are cleared of their inconsistencies and presented in clear and startling nakedness. In many respects, his is an almost ideal character for a philosopher. There is his absolute freedom from Theological prepossession, which enabled him to discuss, without any anxiety about the issue, the successive difficulties of Philosophy, and accept with composure the sceptical conclusion. There is the literary vanity—the last infirmity of philosophic minds—which led him to suppress his earlier work, and suggested brilliant paradox and intolerant posturing against Dogmatists and Mystics; and there is the literary strategy and skill which taught him how to arrange his arguments to win his reader's ears. Perhaps, too, must be added the characteristic frankness with which he confessed that his doubts left him, as soon as he left his study*—the unconscious testimony to the dis-

---
* "Treatise," Bk. IV., sec. vii.

satisfaction which is the natural issue of such a system, and to the obdurate refusal of knowledge to commit such suicide, as Hume recommended. These merits enabled him to see more clearly than ever was seen before the real problem which he had to solve. The problem—forced upon him by preceding thought—was this: given the mind as "a tabula rasa," a passive receptacle of experience, to explain the progress of knowledge. Locke was inclined to fall back on an exterior matter, to be the cause of our sensations and the progressive source of experience. But if all that we can be sure of is sensation, abstract unperceivable Matter is of course an impossible conception. Berkeley was inclined to fall back on Spirit and God, as the fountain-head of knowledge; but the same line of argument, which disposed of Matter apart from a series of sensations, was equally fatal to Mind, or God, apart from a series of sensations. And so the cherished illusions of his predecessors—whether Locke's real primary qualities of a real Matter, or Berkeley's " Spirits " and " God," are dissolved in the glowing crucible of Hume's logic. The conclusion stands forth in naked clearness—that all we can be sure of in consciousness, is just the sensations experienced, and the copies of them in so-called ideas. Such is the " pars destruens " of Hume's work. Let us now remind ourselves, constructively, of the main positions of his system.

1. All knowledge is resolved into sensuous impres-

sions and ideas—the ideas being the copies of the impressions. If then we wish to find the reality of any idea that we have in our minds, we must find the sensuous impression of which it is the copy. In this Hume shows himself a true disciple of the school of Locke.

A double limitation of knowledge is thus introduced. In the first place, knowledge cannot be, in any true sense, *objective*: for as to the original of the sensuous impression we can say nothing. We cannot speak of a Matter, or a Material World, impressing our sense-organs, for this is to travel beyond our record. We are strictly limited to our own perceptions and feelings. In the second place, knowledge cannot be, in any true sense, *subjective*, that is, we cannot put any faith in the constructive power of the mind. For an idea is only so far valid as it is the copy of a sensuous impression. Thus the mind is strictly receptive—working up, with more or less advantage, the materials of sense-impression, in accordance with certain associative principles. So ruthlessly does Hume sweep away Physics and Metaphysics.

2. What are these associative principles? They are three in number: Resemblance, Contiguity in Time and Place, and Causation. The mind is inclined to class together ideas or impressions, which resemble each other, or which occur in close juxtaposition, or

which follow each other so as to lead us to infer that one is the cause of the other.

It is the last of these of which we obviously make most use in constructing our knowledge of the world in which we live: it is the principle of Causality, therefore, which seems to be most objectively real, and it is to this that Hume's attention is most directed.

3. Knowledge, in the opinion of Hume, may be either analytic or synthetic: in other words, we may either get to a clearer comprehension of our own ideas, or attain to fresh additions to our knowledge. Geometrical axioms are instances of analytical knowledge. When we say that two straight lines cannot inclose a space, we are merely analysing what we mean by a straight line, the predicate of the proposition affirming explicitly what was implicit in the subject. Moreover, here we get to a connection which is a necessary one, because we are only moving amongst our own ideas. The contradictory of an analytic proposition (such as the principle that "everything is either A or not A," or the equality of the three angles of a triangle to two right angles), is impossible and absurd. Here then is a "necessity," but merely because we are concerned with the agreement or disagreement of our ideas.

The question is whether synthetic propositions, (propositions which add something to our knowledge,) can ever be necessary. Now reasoning on matters of fact depends principally on the relation of Cause and Effect.

Have we here a necessary connection or not? If it is a necessary connection, the contradictory of an assertion of such relation is absurd and unintelligible. But the assertion that day is not followed by night is certainly not unintelligible. Further, if it is a connection which we attain to *a priori*, we ought, by a mere analysis of the cause, to be able to arrive at the effect. Let us analyse, then, "fire." Can we, by mere analysis, arrive at the knowledge that it gives light? Or, by the analysis of one billiard-ball, can we arrive at the conclusion that, if propelled against another, it will make that other move?

4. The principle of Causality, then, is not a necessary connection, nor is it an *a priori* law of our minds. Of what, then, is it a product? Simply of *experience*. Experience tells us that one thing is followed by another. Further than this we may not go.

5. But by what right, then, do we, as a matter of fact, on the occurrence of one sense-impression, infer that it will be followed by another? We evidently do this, as our every-day experience testifies. What is the justification of this inference? Habit, Custom, answers Hume. We have had many experiences; many experiences produce a certain feeling of expectancy: this is the product of Custom. Hence, on the occurrence of one thing, we infer that it will be followed by another, because we are accustomed or habituated to their conjunction. The notion of a hidden tie, linking together cause and effect, or the idea of Power, is explained as

being nothing else but an expectation grounded on custom. "Power" could only be a valid idea, if we could find its original, *i.e.*, the sensuous impression of which it is a copy. Can we find such a sensuous impression? We cannot, either in the world outside us—for all that we there get is "sequence"—or in the world within us—for all that we are conscious of within us is a flux of sensations and ideas : and neither in the so-called power of the soul over the body, or the power of the Will, is there anything like it. So the "hidden tie," between cause and effect, and the "power" of the Cause to produce the Effect, are only mental hallucinations. So-called "necessary connection," is merely habitual or customary association.

We need not pursue Hume's philosophy any further. We have seen that it rests on the characteristic grounds of empirical Philosophy—grounds which allow of no active or originative power to the mind, and which trace back all human knowledge to sense-impressions. Thus to Hume, the only possible sources of mental possession are "impressions of sense" and "impressions of reflection," or, in other words, sensations and emotions. From these arise in a fainter form ideas,—ideas, which may be on the one hand, the direct heritage of decaying sensations, or, on the other, the product of emotional states, such as "desire," or "aversion."

With this groundwork Hume makes short work of Locke's external matter, and Berkeley's objective and subjective Spirit. In examining his philosophy, we are therefore freed from all necessity of showing how little the world, as a totality of phenomena, or Self-Consciousness, as a totality of feelings and ideas, or God, as the Absolute and Divine Self-Consciousness, can be constructed on such a narrow foundation. We have already seen that Hume, pushing Locke to his logical conclusions, did away with the Primary Qualities of Matter, and Cause, as an objective relation, and performing the same service to Berkeley, showed the non-existence of a Self, and a God.

What difficult problems then remain, which Hume's philosophy of negation or scepticism has to solve? What of the higher questions of Logic and Metaphysics urgently require to be dealt with and cleared up, if the sensationalist or empirical foundation of philosophy is to be accepted?

Sensationalism, not being absolute Pyrrhonism, (or absolute denial of the possibility of knowledge,) has at least to find room for the exact sciences, and the physical sciences. Now Mathematics, broadly speaking, depend on certain ultimate ideas;—*Number, Quantity, Space, Time;* and Physics depend, in their turn, on certain ultimate ideas, such as *the Uniformity of Nature, the conception of Cause and Effect.* Further, the possibility of these ultimate ideas is found itself to depend on prior mental conditions, e.g., *The Faculty of Abstraction* (the formation of general ideas), and *the power of Association of Ideas*, which, in their ultimate expression, amount to the power of forming *Mental Relations*, distinct from and above the changing impressions of sense.

It may easily be gathered that Hume's treatment of these problems was not wholly satisfactory, and that the burden he left to posterity was the re-consideration and re-construction of our notions on these points. Of this Mill himself is not unconscious, though his relation to these questions is peculiar. Mathematics and Physics—these must be saved at all hazards; these must be placed on a foundation, safe from the critical scepticism of Hume. And so it is exactly on these points—on the question of the foundations of Mathematics, and the question of Causation and Natural Uniformity — that Mill differs from his predecessor. But the groundwork is left by Mill undisturbed. Sensationalism and Empiricism are still the dogmatic foundations of his creed. He saw that Hume's treatment of Science and Mathematics was not eminently satisfactory, and so, as we shall hereafter see, he tried to re-mould it. He did *not* see that that treatment followed with rigid consistency from the essential groundwork of the Empirical and Sensational structure, which would itself retaliate on his " re-construction." The character of Mathematical Necessity, and the definition of Cause are very differently stated in Mill and Hume: but the real dependence of these on the prior condition of Mental relations, and the impossibility of any reconstruction of them, unless the notion of Mental action was first re-constructed—to this Mill is characteristically blind. This is just that *lateral oscillation* of which any system is capable in the hands of a disciple. Widen the edifice, but leave the foundation as it is— this is the procedure of Mill, a procedure which is not and cannot be an improvement, but far more probably the cause of future disaster and downfall.

Hume describes himself as "a moderate sceptic."[*] He is right. For there is one thing which he assumes and takes for granted, as an ultimate fact, the validity of which is left to depend on itself. This is "Experience." For if experience be explained by causality, and causality be explained by custom, and custom be explained by experience, we move in a vicious circle, and do not advance one jot in our explanation. Experience is presupposed in the account of experience: experience is explained by experience. So Hume is not a true sceptic, or rather let us say that he is not a true critical philosopher. For a critical philosophy must not take experience for granted, but must seek to explain it. This Kant saw. The line of development of Philosophic Thought runs

[*] "Enquiry," xii., 3.

through Locke and Berkeley and Hume, but Mill is not the successor thereof. The real inheritor of Hume's philosophy, the real disciple, the next great "moment" in the Intellectual advance is not Mill, but Kant.

CHAPTER III.

THE ANTECEDENTS OF MILL—(*continued*).

EIGHTY or ninety years elapsed between Hume's capital work and Mill's. Hume died in 1776. The years of Mill's life fall between 1806—1873. The question, then, naturally suggests itself, what phases of philosophic thought successively appeared in the interval? What systems arose, which presenting and enforcing new points of view, could not help leaving their traces on any thinker of the latter half of the nineteenth century? Such is our present problem.

It was natural that Hume's sceptical tenets should produce an immediate reaction. It was equally natural that the reaction should take two forms, one of which should be the normal rebound against an extreme tension of thought, the other the truer development and expansion by means of criticism and a sounder analysis. The first was to be found in Hume's native country, the second in Germany. The form which the English reaction took in the hands of Reid, Dugald Stewart and Brown, in reality showed a want of philosophic grasp and insight. For, instead of boldly attaching themselves to the analysis of experience (of which Hume made such capital), instead of attempting to see what elements were involved in the phenomena of sensation, perception, and the formation of conceptions, and so arriving at a truer interpretation of the meaning of "experience," the immediate antagonists of Hume fell back upon the verdict of Common Sense, and the somewhat crude notions of what is called "Realism." A beneficial result, which was perhaps a fortuitous consequence of the "Common Sense" stand-point, was the beginning of an independent investigation of psychology, destined to bear greater fruit, when it came into the hands of James Mill and those whom he influenced. According to the views of this reactionary Scotch school, we are *immediately* conscious of external objects and an external world.

The Scotch school were not unfruitful in the History of Philosophy. In France, a school that mingled, in about equal proportions, fragments of Cartesian thought, a nebulous spiritualism and an unedifying eclecticism, carried on the crusade against the spirit of the age, which had been taught to Royer-Collard by Reid. As the Common-Sense School had a horror of Hume, so the French Eclectics had a horror of Condillac and Diderot. Just as Reid and Brown revolted from critical scepticism and atheism, so, under the feverish rhetoric of Victor Cousin, lurked a nervous dread of the Revolutionary spirit.

So far, then, we find a reaction against Hume and Sensationalism, animated, indeed, by the best of motives, but deficient in such metaphysical ability and insight, as are necessary to meet the acute speculations of men like Hume and the Encyclopædists. If the results of philosophical analysis were such a melancholy reversal of current notions and ordinary beliefs, it were better, in the opinion of the reactionists, to give up analysis, and fall back on the broad uncritical methods of the common consciousness. If ordinary men of the world found, notwithstanding the scepticism of Hume, that their wonted views of the world outside them, and the soul inside them, were satisfactory, the fault must lie with the philosopher, and not with their views. Perish philosophical analysis, if its result be scepticism! Such a reaction as this is not singular in the History of Thought, but it has had, and can have but one issue. Analysis can only be conquered by a more perfect analysis: philosophy can only succumb to a truer philosophy. Uncritical oratory only disguises the wounds, which it cannot heal. Rhetoric is oftener the privilege of weakness, than the conscious overflow of power.

The true development of Hume's thoughts came from Germany. Woke from "dogmatic slumber" by Hume, Kant, and after him Fichte, Schelling, and

Hegel, have not only materially altered the conditions of all philosophic thought and inquiry, but have perhaps made more positive contributions to Metaphysical Science than have been made in any one period since the time of Socrates, Plato, and Aristotle.

It is impossible to characterise the work of Kant by a single expression. Coming after Hume and the English school with its two characteristics of Individualism and Sensationalism, Kant saw that the whole ground-work of Human Knowledge must be gone over anew. Nothing short of a revolution in mode and method, it was his claim to have inaugurated. "Critical" is the title given to his philosophy, and critical is throughout its character. For it set itself to analyse the antecedent conditions of experience, the conditions which render that very experience, which was clung to with such fervour by the English school, possible at all. And so Kant's positive result is the discovery that in the whole process of knowledge, from the earliest beginnings of Sensation, there is an interaction of two factors, one of which is supplied by the mind in the so-called "forms," the other supplied by an external element, of which all we can say is, that it is not mental... Critical again the Kantian philosophy is, in the affirmation that we can only deal with phenomena, not with noümena, that what Mind and Spirit are in themselves we cannot say, any more than we can say what Matter is in itself. We are limited to phenomena, the component result of two factors, one objective, the other subjective.

Idealism in one form or other is the character of the philosophy that succeeded Kant: but it is idealism in different phases, and conceived in different ways. Fichte's philosophy, if summed up in a word, is Subjective Idealism, Schelling's is Objective Idealism, Hegel's is Absolute Idealism. This is all the development and carrying out of that one side of the Kantian philosophy which showed itself in the mental forms, *a priori* conceptions, and categories. Another school of German thought attempted to develope the objective side, but with them we are not concerned.

Two other phases of thought appeared in the interval between Hume and Mill, which we must briefly notice. The first of these was inaugurated by Comte and Positivism. Positivism is at once a system of thought, and a system of life, and has contributed alike to logical and social science. With the form of socialism, which is connected with Positivism, we have got nothing to do. But the chief features of Positivism, as a philosophy, are the suppression of all researches beyond phenomena, the affirmation of a great historic law of Progress, and a classification of the Sciences.

Lastly, we must notice an English Psychological School (generally connected with Utilitarianism in

Morals) which immediately preceded and was contemporary with Mill. It commenced with Hartley, was taken up by James Mill, and carried on by Stuart Mill, Alexander Bain, and Herbert Spencer. The chief characteristic of this Psychological School is the stress it lays upon the principle of Association of Ideas, which is its key to the explanation of all mental phenomena.

Here then we have five schools—the Common Sense School, the French Eclectics, the German Metaphysicians, the Positivists, and the English Psychologists, whose influence on Mill we have now to attempt to discover. It will be better, at whatever penalty of methodical dulness, to take each of these in order.

One of them we may at once begin by dismissing. The tendencies of the French Eclectics are utterly alien to that scientific spirit, which is the best element of Mill. They emphasized just those features in their predecessors, which are least connected with the scientific spirit. For the French school of Royer-Collard and others is animated by two principles, Eclecticism and Spiritualism, and Mill is as far from the first as he is from the last.

The influence, however, of the Common Sense School upon Mill is real, though, being indirect, it is by no means easy to define. That system which regards Nature as the exhibition of laws, which are invariable, and which combine to form what we call the "Uniformity of Nature,"—which holds, further, that these laws and uniformities are attainable by the human intellect, while yet it strenuously denies that they are realities, because formed by thought and because in and through them Consciousness is intelligibly constructing the impressions given by the senses—that system, I say, depends for its metaphysical foundation on the doctrines of Realism. And so far as Mill adopts these uniformities of Nature without regarding them as the product of Thought, and conceives that in perception and knowledge we are immediately in contact with a world outside us, (whence it results that Induction and the four Experimental Methods are valid and trustworthy,) so far Mill is at one with that spirit of Realism, which is the animating impulse of the Common Sense School. But, fortunately or unfortunately, Mill's metaphysical foundations, when he discloses them, are not those of Realism. He would call them "Psychological;" we may perhaps be allowed to call them "Idealistic." The so-called Psychological Theory of Matter insists, in the strongest manner, upon the Relativity of our knowledge of the External World; in other words, that Consciousness cannot transcend itself, and that we are and can be only conscious of our own subjective interpretation of things, and not conscious of things in themselves. The conclusion follows with Mill that we cannot apprehend Matter and Objective Reality immediately, but mediately. And further, we cannot apprehend Spirit and Subjective Reality immediately but mediately. In these conclusions, then, Mill is in antagonism to the School of Common Sense. That school would say that the World outside us and the Soul inside us are matters of direct presentation. Mill holds that they are matters of indirect presentation. And so, while allowing, or at least seeming to allow, the scientific conclusions of the Realistic spirit of the Common Sense School, he denies their metaphysical foundation. The influence, in fact, of this school upon Mill is filtered through channels of Brown and Hamilton, and while Brown is, in many respects, by Mill admired and imitated, Hamilton, as the compound of Kant and the Common Sense School, is ruthlessly attacked.

The next school alluded to was formed by the metaphysical systems of Germany. In relation to these it is one of the singular characteristics of Mill that he knows or cares very little about them. He is for ever under the impression that the whole German world is groaning and travailing in the chains of a false metaphysical method: while it is plain to every modern historian of philosophy that Germany is at present leading the whole world even in empirical research. More than this. He makes a startling remark about Kant. The only part, he thinks, of Hume's doctrine about Causality, which "his great adversary Kant" contested, was that Cause meant "the invariable antecedent." Now surely, as a matter of fact, the result of Hume's analysis of Cause was to show that, as it rested upon mere custom, it was variable, or at all events, not objectively invariable: while the result of Kant's analysis was above all this —that Causation was necessary and invariable as being dependent on a mental Category, which made it real (for Reality was the work of Thought) and objectively valid.*

The truth is that Mill, in Idealism, never got beyond such Idealism as is to be found in Berkeley, which is not in reality Idealism at all, or, at most, is subjective Idealism. More accurately, it would be called Sensationalism, qualified by foregone Theological conclusions. It is Sensationalism, so far as the human Consciousness is considered as a merely sentient consciousness, and not a thinking one. It is Idealism, so far as, the analysis being imperfect, Thought, Spirit, Soul, God are instinctively, though not logically, retained.

But Idealism, such as Berkeley's, would never lead Mill to the understanding of Kant, much less of Hegel. He is quite indignant with the German metaphysicians on this ground—that they made mere con-

* Cf. Dr. Stirling, 'Supplementary Notes' to Schwegler's History of Philosophy, p. 455.

ceptions of mind take the place of things. He is in such a hurry to establish this, that he never stops to think whether his own doctrines (as exhibited, *e.g.*, in the Psychological Theories of Matter and Mind) would permit him to consider " things " as anything more than the construction of mind. Assumptions of noumena he cannot away with; yet he too, when pressed, has to admit that things in themselves may exist, though we do not know exactly what they are, because we only know them through their sensations— the very doctrine of Kant.

We shall perhaps better understand the position of Mill when we understand his great obligations and his consequent adherence to the English Psychological School, which immediately preceded him. That school really began with Hartley. The characteristic doctrine of Hartley was his theory of " vibrations "—the doctrine, namely, that all nervous actions, as well as the phenomena of light, heat, and electricity, consist of vibrations, an hypothesis by which he further explained the processes of sensation. But the doctrine which most influenced his successors, was that insistence on the Law of Mental Association, which made Mill call him "the First Father of Association." It was in this that his influence upon Mill was most decided.

James Mill carried out and elaborated the doctrine of Association which he had derived from Hartley, and which has been completed not only by Mill, but much more by Bain and Herbert Spencer. The imperfections of Mr. James Mill have been so well stated by his son in his Preface to the "Analysis of the Phenomena of the Human Mind,"* that I may reproduce two of them here. "First, the imperfection of physiological science at the time at which his book was written. Secondly, a certain impatience of detail and a consequent love of simplification which cannot always be trusted." For instance, the laws of Association of Ideas are reduced to the one principle of contiguity in space and time, (whereas even Hume allowed, as we have seen, of three,) a simplification which Stuart Mill says is "perhaps the least successful in the work." †

The tendency towards physiology and the stress laid on Mental Association, as the source and origin of all Mental Ideas, are the two elements which Mill principally derived from his father and from Hartley, and both will explain his expressed abhorrence of metaphysics. With regard to the first, however, there is this much to be said, that the early disciples of the Association School—James Mill and, to a large extent, Stuart Mill—did not connect their speculations with biology in the same explicit way in which the later advocates of the doctrine do. The dependence of our moral and spiritual nature on our physical nature is the result of the later English psychologists, Bain, Spencer, and George Henry Lewes.

* Vol. i. p. xv. to p. xx.   † Ibid, note 35.

We turn finally to the Positive School and Comte, and we have to ask how far Mill is indebted to that system which Comte inaugurated. The relation of Mill to Positivism is by no means so easy to discuss as the relations we have already examined, nor is it easy to give very decided opinions on the point. A good many of the opponents of Mill have a tendency to merge him in the wider doctrines of Positivism: on the other hand, Mill himself seems inclined to repudiate the connection, and in his book "Auguste Comte and Positivism" delivers some trenchant criticisms on this particular School.

The Positive System is the product we find at once of the positive sciences, and of Saint-Simonism, a combination of empiricism and socialism. The latter element we have agreed to drop out of the consideration; and, indeed, some of the speculations of M. Comte on this point have been repudiated by his best modern followers—M. Littré and others.

Further, there are two sides to Positivism. There is the destructive side, wherein we find the search for final causes and first causes is distinctly abandoned. With the beginning and end of things we have nothing to do, we are only concerned with what lies between these two extremes. Thus all forms of theology, all forms of metaphysics, are practically discarded.

Now, so far as this point is concerned, it is undoubtedly true that much the same truly positive standpoint must be ascribed to Mill. He too is a phenomenalist, an empiricist: one who relies on experience to find laws of co-existence, and does not busy himself with more than the middle levels of knowledge, eliminating all transcendental researches. On the other hand, it is none the less true that this aspect of things is by no means confined to Positivism; nor can Comte claim to have been its author or expounder. As Mill himself says in " Comte and Positivism," " The Philosophy called Positivism is not a recent invention of M. Comte, but a simple adherence to the traditions of all the great scientific minds whose discoveries have made the human race what it is." That is to say, Positivism is only a particular form of the modern scientific spirit—that spirit which had its rise in Descartes and Newton, and animated all the men of science. But though Mill thus agrees with the range of subjects proposed for inquiry, he does not quite, like Comte, abandon metaphysical speculation altogether—witness many of his chapters in "An Examination of Hamilton." Moreover, with regard to the fundamental questions of knowledge—the whence and the whither—Mill is not so truculent as Comte; he says, that " it is a mistake on the part of M. Comte to leave no open questions." He says again, that " the positive mode of thinking is not necessarily a negation of the supernatural." This is an important qualification of Mill's agreement with the destructive side of Positivism.

Beside the destructive side, however, there is a constructive side to Positivism which shows itself in two main positions.

(i.) The historic conception—the "loi des trois états"—that the human mind necessarily passes through three stages, the theological, the metaphysical, and the positive.

(ii.) The co-ordination of the Sciences—a hierarchy of arrangement,—in which each later or more complex science depends on the one above it, and each additional complexity has to be met by new devices in experimental inquiry. And the order is, Mathematics, Astronomy, Physics, Chemistry, Biology, and Sociology.

Now, with regard to the first of these, Mill appears in the main to accept it.* With regard to the second, however, there is more antagonism on the part of Mill. He notices omissions from the Scheme—Logic, for instance, and Political Economy. But the gravest omission is Psychology. Comte expressly repudiates Psychology, and for him the only way to arrive at the results at which Psychology aims, is to pursue Physiology, or some improved kind of Phrenology. Here Mill, as the true descendant of a Psychological School, is up in arms. He points out in answer to Comte's criticisms that the mind can attend to a great number of impressions at once; that the mind can study some of its own phenomena by the aid of memory; and that

* "Comte and Positivism," p. 33.

Psychology is much further advanced than that portion of physiology which corresponds to it.*

We find, in fact, that Comte's attack on Psychology is not supported by Comtists, *e.g.*, Littré and Lewes. It had, however, its effect in leading to the substitution of a study of minds in history, in the place of an exclusively individual introspection—to a larger interpretation of experience than the merely individual experience which formed the staple of Psychology before. But now it is not doubted that Psychology is a science; the only question is whether it should be considered a part of Biology, or hold an independent place after Biology and before Ethology, as with Mill.†

Lastly, with regard to Sociology itself, Mill refuses to allow that the merit of its acknowledgment as a science belongs to Comte.‡ "He has not created Sociology." The reason of this, in Mill's eyes, is that Sociology depends on Ethology, and Ethology on Psychology, and Comte did not do justice either to Ethology or Psychology. But Mill's assertion is perhaps too sweeping. Anyone who compares Mill's chapters on Sociology,§ with Comte's "Philosophie Positive," will see that without the foundation of Comte Mill's edifice would never have been reared. Yet still, perhaps, there is some truth in the assertion

---

* Mill's "Logic," vol. ii., b. vi., c. iv. "Comte and Positivism," p. 67.
† "Logic," b. vi.
‡ "Comte and Positivism," pp. 70 and 130.   § "Logic," bk. vi.

that that part of the new science of Sociology which is "Statics" must be referred to Aristotle as its author, while that which is "Dynamics" is nothing more than the historic law of evolution discussed above. But Comte's application of the law of evolution to a Philosophy of History seems to Mill to have been a great achievement.

Such is the result of an analysis of Mill's relations to Comte and Positivism, which, perhaps, unduly lessens his obligations; for, after all, the formulator and systematiser of a particular point of view deserves to be called, in a certain sense, an inventor, and the man who comes after him finds his work materially lightened. What Mill himself says of his obligations to Comte is perhaps too absolutely put.* "My work is indebted to Comte for several important ideas, but a short list would exhaust the chapters and even the pages which contain them."

In concluding this general review of the interval which elapsed between Hume and Mill, and of Mill's relations to the successive schools of thought which appeared in the interval, we may, perhaps, venture upon a generalisation. Mill is the product of Hume, Hartley, and Comte. He is indebted to Hume for Sensationalism, and to Hartley for his Associationalism, while, in accordance with Comte, he adopts Phenomenalism.

* "Examination of Hamilton," ch. xiv., p. 266, note 2.

In many ways, however, it is Herbert Spencer, and not Mill, who is the true culmination of this school. For instead of merely accepting the associational psychology, he has merged it in the broader law of evolution. The doctrine of the development of psychical states out of inseparable associations, is only a special example of the great law of Evolution. This universal doctrine of evolution Herbert Spencer has sought to apply, not only to the development of all forms of being, whether material or spiritual, but to the evolution of the relations necessary to knowledge. Thus, so-called *a priori* conditions of knowledge are shown to be the results of the development of experience in the race.

In modern times the experimental school of Philosophy has widened itself in many directions. Besides the application of the conception of Evolution, and the larger interpretation of Psychology, which we have already noticed, there is a profounder study of Biology, and the beginnings of an appreciation of the results of Philological labours (as, *e.g.*, in Mr. Morell). James Mill saw the importance of this point, but his philology is, of course, antiquated, being based on nothing better than Horne Tooke. These results are due in large measure to the influence of the better elements of Positivism, and to the labours in Germany of Herbart, Fechner, and Helmholtz. The English writers to whom I principally refer are Bain, Spencer, Lewes, Carpenter, Maudsley, Darwin, Morell, and Sully.

CHAPTER IV.

CONSCIOUSNESS.

MILL himself says that he abjures Metaphysics. In speaking of his relations to Comte and Positivism, he says that he agrees with the position of that school, so far as it rejects First Causes and Final Causes; his only concern being with "Physical" Causes. But he too is a Psychologist—one of those men through whose labours, as he says, rather grandiloquently, "The Sceptre of Psychology has decidedly returned to England." And in the foundations on which his Psychology rests, he has to deal with metaphysics, and with those questions on which metaphysics claims to be heard. A passage from his "Examination of Sir William Hamilton's Philosophy"* contains explicitly this avowal. "England is often reproached by continental Thinkers with indifference to the higher philosophy. But England did not always deserve this reproach, and is already showing by no doubtful symptoms that she will not deserve it much longer. Her

* "Examination," p. 2, the references throughout are to the 3rd edition.

thinkers are again beginning to see, what they had only temporarily forgotten, that a true Psychology is the indispensable scientific basis of Morals, of Politics, of the science and art of Education : that the difficulties of metaphysics lie at the root of all science : that those difficulties can only be quieted by being resolved, and that until they are resolved, positively whenever possible, but at any rate negatively, we are never assured that any human knowledge, even physical, stands on solid foundations." No clearer or franker avowal could be made by one who is often, though inaccurately, called an English Positivist.

The first of these metaphysical questions is undoubtedly concerned with " Consciousness." Here again Mill is explicit. " When we know," he says, " what any philosopher considers to be revealed in Consciousness, we have the key to the entire character of his metaphysical system." * By Mill's own invitation, then, we have to consider what he believes to be revealed in Consciousness ; though, to a great extent, we can only gain this indirectly by discovering his own opinions from his criticisms on Hamilton. Three chapters in his " Examination "—" The Relativity of Knowledge," " Consciousness as understood by Sir W. Hamilton," and " The Interpretation of Consciousness "—will suffice to acquaint us with Mill's opinion on this question. We shall then, after summing up

* " Examination," p. 132.

the main features of that opinion, be able to consider how far it may be considered adequate or satisfactory.

"The Relativity of Human Knowledge" merely means, in its broadest and simplest statement, that we know no more of external objects than what the senses tell us. But the doctrine itself may be held in two different forms. We may either mean that not only are the sensations all that we can possibly know of the objects, but all that we have any ground for believing to exist. Or else, without committing ourselves to such extreme Idealism, we may only wish to signify by the doctrine that, while the Ego and the Non-Ego are undoubtedly realities, yet that they are for us unknowable, because all that we know about them are the impressions they make upon us. A further discrimination can, however, be made between two varieties of opinion, contained in the last form of the statement. According to one school, we have in Consciousness, over and above sensations *plus* an unknowable cause, certain forms of sense and categories of the understanding (*e.g.*, Time, Space, Substantiality, Causality, &c.) which are modes under which we are forced to represent to ourselves Things-in-themselves. According to another school, these conceptions of Time, Space, Substance, and Cause are not innate forms of the mind, but merely " conceptions put together out of ideas of *sensation*, by the known laws of Association." It is, of course, to this last expression of the doctrine, that being admitted to be without appeal, the question naturally arises, *To what* does Consciousness bear witness? Hamilton draws a distinction between " the facts given in the act of consciousness " which must remain undoubted, and "the facts, to the reality of which it only bears evidence," which have been largely doubted by the majority of Philosophers. This, says Mill, is a mis-statement of the question at issue. For it is not questioned whether the facts testified to by consciousness are true, but whether consciousness does actually testify to them at all. It is not that the testimony is undoubted, and the *veracity* of the testimony called in question, but whether consciousness is ever witness to anything beyond itself. As a matter of fact, Philosophers have not disputed the veracity of consciousness, but rather the fact of its testimony. Nor is this absurd. Substitute for " consciousness," the words " intuitive knowledge," and it is at once clear that intuition itself will not tell us what knowledge is intuitive. It is therefore quite open to doubt whether consciousness does or does not affirm any given thing, although at first sight such a doubt appears impossible. The question " what do we know intuitively," or " to what does our consciousness testify," is, then, not a matter of simple self-examination, ˙   ˙ science. There are two methods, Mill conti˙   in which the question is sought to be solv   he first, the Introspective Method, attempts by carefully sifting our present states of consciousness to pronounce those to be ultimate and primary truths, which we cannot by our analysis resolve into something simpler. But inasmuch as the laws of Mind are capable of constructing some conceptions which become so identified with all our consciousness that we cannot but think them intuitive, this process appears to be unsafe. The only way is to discover what truths there are in the mind, whose origin cannot in any reasonable way be accounted for. When, after a study of the modes of generation of the mental facts confessedly not original, we have applied the same process to those which are supposed to be original, then only can we say that the phenomena, which remain unaccounted for by those modes of generation, are primary and original elements of the mind. This is the true psychological method, and Locke, says Mill, was right in laying the main stress upon the "origin of our ideas."

If now we add to the foregoing Mill's theories of Mental Association, the device by which the growth of our Ideas out of sensations is to be explained, we shall have exhausted the whole content of "Consciousness" according to Mill. Hume, we remember, enunciated three principles, according to which ideas were associated: Resemblance, Contiguity, and Causation.

According to Mill the Law of Association has

four exemplifications.* Ideas are associated through Similarity, and through Contiguity (which may be equivalent either to Simultaneity or Immediate Succession). The two remaining laws run as follows: "Increased certainty is given by repetition to Ideas associated by contiguity," and "the inseparability of the Associated Ideas is transferred to the facts answering to them." The characteristic properties of the Law are that the suggestions they produce are for the time irresistible, and that the suggested ideas (at least when the association is of the synchronous kind as distinguished from the successive) become so blended together by a species of "mental chemistry," † that the compound result appears to our consciousness simple. Secondary actions of the Law connect themselves with "laws of obliviscence," and "unconscious mental modifications," ‡ but these we need not here particularly define.

We are now in a position to understand Mill's theory of "Consciousness." Let us try and sum up the main features.

In the first place, we now see with what propriety Mill is classed with the Sensationalist School. For with him, as with them all, man's knowledge is the result—a complex result it is true, but still a result—

---

* "Examination," pp. 219, 220. "Logic," Bk. vi., c. 4.
† Ibid, p. 307.
‡ Ibid, pp. 313, 314, 335, 341—343.

of what he derives from the communications of sense. "He knows nothing more of objects than what the senses tell him." Mill, in fact, expressly disavows any other factor of knowledge in his criticisms of the "pretensions" of the *a priori* school. There are no innate forms or categories of the mind with him. Those notions which are mistaken for such, are, in reality, complex results of certain associations set up among the intimations of sense. Nor yet, according to Mill, can we embrace the alternative opinion—that in sensation we are immediately conscious of objects. We are not so conscious immediately, but only mediately. These objects are not intuitions, they are inferences. Mill, then, is equally the antagonist of the Kantian school, and of the Scotch school of Common-Sense, or Realism. He is a follower, an exponent of that mode of philosophy which was inaugurated by Locke, and carried on by Berkeley and Hume.

All we know, then, in the first and ultimate resort, are Sensations. But with the Sensation, there is something more, Mill thinks, than the momentary modification of the sensibility. There is also the Consciousness of the Sensation. "Sensation and the consciousness of a sensation are one and the same thing." The Sensation, in fact, carries with it, as a component part of itself, or as identical with itself (given seemingly in one act), the Consciousness of the Sensation.

In the third place, ideas, as we have them, are merely worked up (as it were) out of sensations by certain laws of Association. These are the all-powerful instruments of the Psychological school, the potent alchemy by which all sort of unexpected results are made to appear. Thus it comes about that we are possessed of notions, concepts, ideas, of which we can not divest ourselves, which we cannot help applying to things, and which appear to be a necessary part of our thinking processes, but which are, in reality, but "the baseless fabric of a vision." When the Sensation, the Consciousness of a Sensation, and the Laws of Association are enumerated, we have the whole content of Consciousness,—at least on its intellectual side. Phenomena of volition, and phases of emotion do not come within our present scope.

Let us make a few remarks on these three points in turn. The first position is, as Mill points out, common to all those who believe in "the Relativity of knowledge." Berkeley, Kant, and Mill agree in this, that all that we can know of objects is what the senses tell us, *i.e.*, phenomena. The divergence appears later. Is Sensation the only factor in the body, or complex, of our knowledge? Is the whole reality of knowledge to be explained as the mere product of Sense? The *cause* of our Sensations, whatever it may be, must be put out of court, for that is unknowable. Can knowledge, then, be exactly resolved into Sensations, *plus* an unknowable cause, or is there anything more to be said? Does the mind interfere in any way, does it add something to experience, which is not gained from experience? It does, answers Kant, it adds "forms." It does not, answers Mill: what you call "forms" are merely the result of sensation, worked up by purely natural processes of association.*

Knowledge, then, is experience, and experience is sensation, according to Mill. Now in knowledge, there must be some distinction between Reality and Unreality. What is the Real? Why is any object—that chair, say—a *real* object for me? There are two adequate answers, and, so far as I know, only two. You may say, "The object is real for me, because in sensation I am immediately conscious of an object, because I am, in this instance, in immediate contact with objective reality." That is the answer of Common Sense, which, in Philosophy, goes by the name of Realism. Or you may say, "The object is real, because it is the construction of my thought, reality being nothing else than this mental construction. The sensation comes and goes, but my mind fixes it, by bringing it into relation with, and distinguishing it from, everything else, and so it becomes a real part of my knowledge." That is the answer of what may be called Idealism. Mill is precluded from the first answer, because with him, in opposition to Hamilton, we are

* See note at end of Chapter V.

not conscious of objects intuitively. He is precluded from the second answer, because with him the mind does not bring *a priori* relations to bear upon its experience. What then is *real?* The Sensation. Remember, too, that Mill cannot fall back upon the general experience of Humanity, or Universal Sensationalism, because this is just that further contribution made by Spencer to the interpretation of Experience. His position demands that in each man's case his stores of knowledge arise out of the sensations *he* has in past time experienced. "The real," then, is just an individual man's individual personal sensations. A truly Protagorean answer.

It is clear, then, that we must analyse "Sensation," and this leads us to Mill's second position. Sensation is not merely sensation; it is more, it is the Consciousness of a Sensation. Now, in one sense of the words, to say that a sensation and the consciousness of a sensation are one and the same thing, is to utter a truism. It may only be equivalent to saying, "When I feel, I feel," which is obvious and unimportant enough. But, of course, on such a slender foundation as this cannot be reared even the ground-plan of knowledge. In reality this is not what we are intended to infer from the words. The consciousness of a sensation is "the realising" of a sensation; and the realisation, the making a reality of it, means, when we analyse it, the bringing it into relation with, and differentiating it from, any and every other sensation we experience. To be conscious of a sensation means that for us we accept it into the mind as *one thing*, we so regard it as to make it our own, so that we are able to identify it again when it recurs. But a mere sensation cannot of itself (unless, indeed, we accept the doctrines of Realism) make itself different from every other, so that it can be identified when it recurs. How can it? It is but an impression on our sensibility, that sensibility being completely passive, *ex hypothesi*. To raise it from such mere passive impression, to make it real, must be the work of the mind in some way or other (however we name it) going out to it, putting relations on it, and then bringing it into Consciousness as one thing. Now, such "a consciousness of sensation" as this is by no means the same thing as sensation; it is different with all the difference between having and receiving, between activity and passivity.

When Mill, however, says that a sensation and the consciousness of a sensation are one and the same thing, we accept the sentence, unthinkingly, because it strikes us as a truism in the first sense of the words. But, really, to raise out of Sensation the edifice of knowledge, it must be used in the second sense of the words, because only such confusion between sentient and mental acts could lead to the success of the attempt to educe all knowledge out of sensation. Mill gets all the benefit out of the first sense of the words, when really what he must mean is the second sense. But Aristotle knew better, when he discriminated between the separate intimations of sense (ἴδιαι αἰσθήσεις) and something more than mere sense (τὸ δ'ὅτι αἰσθανόμεθα.)*

Nor can such an analysis of the primary acts of sensation be possibly distasteful to Mill. For the whole spirit of his treatment of Hamilton (*e.g.* in the chapter "The interpretation of Consciousness") is just this,—that we must not take what appears to be primary as if it were really such: it may be secondary: it may be complex, and not simple: and only further analysis can tell. And the Experiential Philosopher is, as we have seen, justly sceptical of words like "ultimate" and "primary." So we are quite within the procedure of the proper Psychological method of Mill, when we take such a sentence as "sensation and the consciousness of a sensation are one and the same thing," and see whether such a supposed primary act is, or is not, primary,—whether these two are one and the same thing, or not,—whether "a consciousness of a sensation" is really a simple thing, or a complex thing.

With Mill's successors, the question is solved in a bolder manner. To later exponents of the Psychological method, consciousness in its primitive condition is resolved into two acts, first, the consciousness of a

* De Anima, iii. 1, 2.

difference, then the consciousness of a similarity.* But if sensation at once implies, in one and the same act, the perception of a difference between itself and everything else, what else is this but " consciousness testifying to something other than itself"—" the knowing not only *that* I know, but also *what* I know"—that identical doctrine of Realism, on which, when uttered by Hamilton, Mill pours out all the vials of his scathing criticism?

We come now to the third point, the Laws of Mental Association. In his study of Association, Mill is, perhaps, not so explicit, nor does he embark on so complete a study, as some of his school, notably Bain. Yet the matter is one of paramount importance to him, for by him the idea of cause is reduced to an inseparable, unconditional association, and on cause Mill rests his entire theory of reasoning. That Mill was not unduly insensible to this importance, we may gather from the following sentence: † "That which the Law of Gravitation is to Astronomy, that which the elementary properties of the tissues are to Physiology, the Law of the Association of Ideas is to Psychology."

What that Law includes we have already seen. What we now have to see,—and it is a question to which Mill never addresses himself,—is what such Association

---

* Cf., among others, Bain, "Senses and Intellect," Introduction; and " Emotions and Will," p. 566 and following.

† " Comte and Positivism," p. 53.

implies, what conditions it postulates either in the things that are known or the thing that knows. Such a question, obviously prior to all the exhibitions of the principle such as we have them in Mill, is exactly that which no Sensationalist or Experientialist philosopher handles. And to ignore it means one of two things, either to be a Realist and not a Sensationalist at all, or else to be guilty of a want of analysis in those very intimations of Consciousness which it is the bounden duty of the experimental psychologist (according to Mill) thoroughly to sift and analyse.

What then do we mean by the Association of Sensations and Ideas? What does such a faculty presuppose?

In the first place, it is clear that associating power should naturally belong to a mind that is active* (actively dealing with and transforming sensations) rather than to a mind that is passive (passively receiving such sensations as they successively present themselves). "To associate" is, of course, to do, rather than to suffer, by the very force of the term. Such an objection may appear mere haggling over words, but in reality it leads us to the very core of

---

* Mill was afterwards not insensible to this. Cf. "Dissertations and Discussions," vol. iii., art. on Bain. "Those who have studied the writings of the Association Psychologists, must often have been unfavourably impressed by the almost total absence, in their analytical expositions, of the recognition of any active element as spontaneity in the mind itself" (p. 119).

the question. We shall see this more clearly by addressing ourselves to a second point. " Sensations and the resultant ideas are associated according to certain laws." What does this mean? It means, obviously, that certain sensations being held in consciousness, and their relations, whether of contiguity or resemblance, being apprehended by the mind, they are associated together. Any process less than this would never result in association. Think what association, in popular senses of the word, means. I associate together the idea of this paper with the idea of an essay. That is to say, having received through my senses certain impressions of a particular kind, to which after due consideration I apply the name of paper, I then think of them in relation to other impressions which I call writing or reading an essay. It is clear that if my first impressions had come and gone, and not been retained, fixed, made permanent, made real, by my ever-present consciousness, I could never have thought of them in relation to my second impressions, because they would not have been there to be thought of. In other words, thought has to make sensations real before they can be associated; and, further, they cannot be associated, unless, being made real, they can be identified when they recur.

This is all upon the supposition which Mill himself makes for us when he says (as indeed all Sensationalists must) that all that we can know of things is the sensations we experience. If that is the case, if sensation does not testify to anything beyond itself, then a sensation, on analysis, is discovered to amount to nothing more than a particular impression, out of which, by some further process, knowledge and reality are produced. And then naturally we have to consider, as we have done, whether a sensation has not to be transformed in some way before it can become a permanent item of knowledge; and, further, whether, unless it be thus transformed, it can ever become real enough to be associated with any other sensation.

There is, however, another supposition which is possible. The sensations may come ready-formed, in a certain way, into our mind. As ready-formed, they must have, of course, their similarities to and differences from other sensations already fixed. Then to a mind, purely passive, there would certainly be open the tendency to associate them, for the simple reason that the sensations themselves in their resemblances, naturally and of themselves, tend to coagulate into groups. This supposition I say is possible, but it certainly is not possible for Mill. For what does it imply? That sensations are fixed in a certain objective order. That is, that when we are conscious of sensations, we are not merely limited within the bounds of consciousness, but that we are passively recipient of a certain objective order, obviously *beyond* consciousness. And this means that sensations do not merely imply themselves, but something more than themselves, viz., their relations, their differences, their resemblances, to and from one another. But this is a Hamiltonian doctrine, in other, words, Realism. As such, then, it is not open to Mill.

The conclusion would appear to be this. If Realism be accepted, then Sensations can be associated, because they may be conceived as already existing in a certain objective order: but if Sensationalism be accepted, then Sensations cannot be associated at all, for there must first be a mental process (not "feeling") to bring them into relations with one another, in order that they may be associated. So little is it true that Association explains Thought, that the reverse is the case. It is Thought which explains the possibility of Association.

CHAPTER V.

BODY AND MIND.

AFTER the metaphysical question as to the contents of Consciousness and the extent and validity of its testimony, we come to the equally serious metaphysical difficulties which surround the words "Matter and Body," and "Mind or Self." Here we have very explicit theories on the part of Mill in the two chapters of his "Examination," entitled respectively "The Psychological Theory of the Belief in an External World," and "The Psychological Theory of Matter how far applicable to Mind."* With these theories we must now do our best to acquaint ourselves.

"The Psychological Theory" begins by postulating certain conditions "in nature," and certain conditions in the mind itself. The conditions it postulates in Nature are as follows :—

(i.) Sensations.

(ii.) Succession and simultaneousness of Sensations.

(iii.) The union of these sensations (both successive

* "Examination of Hamilton's Philosophy," Chaps. XI. and XII.

and simultaneous) into groups, so that the experience of one sensation authorises us to expect all the rest, provided that certain antecedent sensations, called organic, are first experienced.

The conditions which the theory postulates in the mind itself are—

(i.) The Law of Expectation and Memory.

(ii.) The Laws of the Association of Ideas (which we have already enumerated).

With these assumptions, the Psychological theory undertakes to prove that the conception of External Matter would necessarily be generated (if it was not an original datum of consciousness) by the known laws of the Mind. The steps in this gradual belief in Externality may be reduced to four:—

1. We have a present sensation, and we conceive of possibilities of sensation (by experience). The possibilities of sensation are *permanent*, while the present sensation is fugitive.

2. The possibility of sensation refers not to a single sensation, but to a group of sensations. Now if I experience one of them, I know I could experience all. Hence the possibilities of sensation are conceived of as permanent, not only in opposition to the temporariness of my bodily presence, but to the temporary character of any one of the sensations, of which the group referred to is composed. Here we observe that the idea of a "substratum" is in process of formation.

3. Experience of an *order* in our sensations leads to the belief in the law of Cause and Effect. Now the antecedent of a sensation is in most cases a possibility of sensation, involving a group of contingent sensations. The Idea of "Cause," therefore, is connected with these permanent possibilities, as are also ideas of "power," "activity," "energy," and the like: and the *actual* sensations are supposed to have a background in the *possibilities* of sensation. The idea of a "substratum" is now fully developed.

4. One more step, and the analysis is complete. We find other people acting on the supposition of these permanent possibilities of sensation as well as ourselves: whereas our actual sensations are not common to our fellow-creatures. The World, then, of Possible Sensations, belonging to other people, as well as to me, is held to constitute an External World.

Such is Mill's extremely acute and subtle analysis of the growth of our belief in Externality. The conclusion is plain. If we ask What is Matter? the only answer which a psychologist can give, is that it is merely "a Permanent Possibility of Sensation." This is all, says Mill, that is essential to the belief in Matter, whether held by philosophers or ordinary humanity.

Can the same analysis be extended to "Mind?" Mill believes that, to a large extent, it can. Just as the Non-Ego might easily have been formed as a conception, by the known laws of the mind, even if it was not in consciousness from the beginning, so also (subject to a somewhat grave difficulty, to which we shall return later) the notion of the Ego, as "a substratum," might have been formed. For it is evident that we have no conception of the Mind, as distinguished from its conscious manifestations, *i.e.*, sensations and internal feelings. The belief in mind, therefore, is nothing more than a belief in a Permanent Possibility of Sequent Feelings. If this be so, what evidence have we, on this hypothesis, of the existence of our fellow-creatures, of the existence of God, of Immortality? Just as much evidence, Mill thinks, as we have on the ordinary theory. We believe, for instance, that our fellow-creatures have minds, because our senses assure us that they have the antecedent conditions for feelings, (bodies,) and the subsequent effects, (acts and outward demeanour.) I know in my own case that the first link produces the last only through the intermediate link of feelings. I infer that this must be the case with them. Now this inference is just as valid on the assumption that neither Mind nor Matter is anything but a permanent possibility of Sensation. I am conscious of my own body, as a group of possible sensations, connected in a peculiar way with all my sensations, and I observe other bodies closely resembling mine, except that they are not so connected. I conclude, therefore, that they are connected with some other than myself, judging from my own experience of my sensations. So, again, these bodies exhibit phenomena, which I know in my case to be the effects of consciousness. Therefore I infer that these other bodies have a consciousness similar to mine.

Similarly, this theory would resolve the Mind of God into a series of Divine thoughts and feelings, prolonged through Eternity, which would cause a belief in it, at least as strong as the belief in my own. And the conception of Immortality, as a thread of consciousness prolonged to Eternity, leads essentially to the same results as the ordinary conception.

But still there remains "a final inexplicability." Besides present feelings and possibilities of feelings, we have Memory and Expectation. But how can a series of feelings be aware of itself as a series, so as to remember a sensation that actually existed in the past, or expect that a particular sensation will exist in the future? Here we are face to face with an insoluble metaphysical problem.* "I think by far the wisest thing we can do, is to accept the inexplicable fact, without any theory of how it takes place. No such difficulties, however, attend the Psychological theory in its application to Matter."

We are now acquainted with the manner in which, according to Mill, by "known laws of the mind" are generated those notions of the World outside us, and

* "Examination," p. 242.

of the Self within us, of which we appear to be so immediately and directly conscious. With Mill, as the preceding analysis will have shown, these are not direct, immediate facts of intuition, but acts of progressive belief, which can be demonstrated to have *grown* to be what they are. It will be convenient, for many reasons, to examine the account of Mind, or Self, first, before proceeding to the treatment of Externality.

"The Self" is by Mill, as a disciple of Hume, duly shown to be but "states of consciousness."* "We neither know nor can imagine it except as represented by the succession of manifold feelings." But what of the permanent something we seem to be conscious of, in contrast with the flux of sensations? This, says Mill (just like the Permanent Substratum we seem to be conscious of with regard to "matter") is wholly covered by the expression "Permanent *Possibility:*" and so, the mind is nothing but a series of Feelings. At the end of the chapter, however, we find that "the permanent something" is not wholly covered by the bare expression "permanent possibility." There is something else—there is *expectation*, and there is *memory*, still unaccounted for. How can a mere series be aware of itself in the past, as in memory, or project itself into the future, as in expectation? Here, says Mill, we are face to face with "a final inexplicability,"

* "Examination," p. 235.

and the wisest thing is to accept the inexplicable fact and be content.

Contentment, however, is not an easy virtue, and we cannot help pausing over this "final inexplicability," which looks so remarkably like a confession of failure by the very words in which Mill states it. Let us turn, for a moment, to the Psychological Theory of the Belief in an External World. What does it postulate according to Mill? It postulates, first, that the human mind is capable of *expectation*.* But expectation, we find, is just that which the theory of mind cannot explain and has to accept as a final inexplicability. Consequently the Theory of the External World rests on a function of the Mind, which the corresponding theory finds itself unable to explain. That is to say, if words have any meaning, that, as the one theory rests on the other, they both rest on a final inexplicability. Yet, says Mill, with almost unparalleled hardihood, "No such difficulties attend the theory in its application to matter." †

Though Mill allows himself here to speak of a "final inexplicability" he will not allow others to do the same. In the earlier part of his "Examination,"‡ he notices with pain that Hamilton had left the relations of Belief and Knowledge unsolved. This he calls "an extremely unphilosophical liberty" to take. The next words are exactly applicable to the present

* "Examination," p. 219.   † Ibid. p. 242.   ‡ Ibid. p. 146.

case.* "But when a thinker is compelled by one part of his philosophy to contradict another part, he cannot leave the conflicting assertions standing, and throw the responsibility of his scrape on the arduousness of the subject. A palpable self-contradiction is not one of the difficulties which can be adjourned, as belonging to a higher department of science." Yet here, notwithstanding these brave words, is an instance of Mill taking an "extremely unphilosophical liberty," precisely similar to that which he reprobates in Hamilton.

Of course, the truth is that Mill has here got hold of that which must be a stumbling-block in Sensational schemes of Philosophy. You reduce Mind to a series of feelings, and then have to answer the pertinent question, How can a series be aware of itself in past and future time? The fact is that such a series can never be summed; and Personal Identity vanishes in the process. And yet Mill says that this theory leaves Immortality just as it was before. "It is precisely as easy to conceive that a succession of feelings, a thread of consciousness, may be prolonged to eternity, as that a spiritual substance continues to exist."† If, indeed, despite the fact of Self being "sequent feelings," Personal Identity remains all the same, perhaps this is conceivable. But the ambiguity lurks in the words "thread" and "succession." If it is "a thread" of

* "Examination," p. 147.   † Ibid. p. 240.

consciousness, it may, of course, be prolonged. But a "thread" means something one and continuous, and Sensations coming and going (sequent feelings) are not one and continuous. "*Successive* feelings" are by no means the same thing as "*a succession* of feelings," despite Mill's assertion* that "we are conscious of a succession, in the fact of having successive sensations." For "*a succession*" of feelings, is only possible to a self-consciousness, which remains constant and identical throughout all the successive sensuous modifications. But a self-consciousness, constant and identical, can never be admitted by Mill.

There is another objection to Mill's account of Mind or Self which is urged by Dr. M'Cosh in his Examination of Mill's Logic, and which furnishes us, at all events, with a fair "argumentum ad hominem." The system, of which Mill is an advocate, aims at assuming as few original principles as possible. Sensationalism, like Nominalism, accepts William of Ockham's maxim, "Entia non multiplicanda sunt præter necessitatem." This is why it wishes to destroy the *a priori* element of knowledge, and postulates only the "*a posteriori*" experience. Let us apply this to our present case.

The old Realistic way of regarding Mind was, of course, to say that we have in our mental modifications, an original and intuitive presentation of Self. In sensation it is always "the Ego having the sensation."

* Appendix, p. 256.

No sensation comes without having, as its uniform accompaniment the consciousness of the Self which feels it. This is, in truth, the position of Dr. McCosh—that in Self, we have an immediate presentation or intuition. Mill would replace this by something more scientific. Instead of the Self, then, one and immediate, what have we according to Mill? First, we have Sensations; then a series of Sensations; then we have a belief; then, a belief in Time; then a belief in Time as permanent, and of possibilities in Time.* These are obviously not all one and the same, yet they are all seemingly ultimate elements. So that instead of one ultimate element, as in Realism, we have got five or six. This is hardly in accordance with the spirit of Ockham.

Somewhat different is the conclusion to which Idealism commits itself in the hands of Kant. Of course, like all those who admit the essential Relativity of Human Knowledge, he must say that what the Mind is in itself we cannot say, any more than we can say what Matter is in itself. The Self or Mind can only be known by its own Forms, its Categories, its Relations. Apart from such relations and forms, no human knowledge, we find, is possible. Now, the application of permanent categories and relations is of course necessarily a limitation of know-

* The sentence in Mill is (p. 241) :—" They are attended with the peculiarity that each of them involves a belief in more than its own present existence," *i.e.* a permanent belief of possible sensations in the future. Here is Time implicit in the earliest operations of consciousness

ledge; it is just that which makes it Relative instead of Absolute.

Again, human knowledge can only exist as a joint effect of two opposite factors, Object and Subject. Consequently, there cannot be knowledge of merely one of the component factors. Thus what Self is in itself must for ever remain unknown.

But this is not the same thing as reducing Self to Sequent Sensations as Sensationalism does. For observe that we know the Self by the permanency of the relations, which it applies in the construction of its experience. Permanent mental categories mean, of course, as we have all along said, a permanent Self-Consciousness, ever present as one and identical to all the impressions of sense, transmuting and transforming them out of the bewildering flux into the constant conditions of knowledge. It is thus that Self-Consciousness and Self are assured by an *a priori* system of metaphysics.

To some of the successors of Kant, this limitation of our knowledge of Self seems unnecessary and unreal. Of Self we ought to have an absolute consciousness—differentiating itself, as in the categories, returning again upon itself as in the conclusions of a rational Psychology. " It is an unity in difference, an unity which can only be known in difference, but still an unity." *

* "The Philosophy of Kant," by Edward Caird, pp. 481, 484, 553, 558.

What is Matter, External Reality, Objective World, to Mill? It is defined as "the Permanent Possibility of Sensation." What are the conditions postulated in arriving at this result? Three in the mind: *viz.*, Expectation, Memory, and the Laws of Association: three in " nature " : *viz.*, Sensations, Succession or Simultaneousness of Sensations, and the union of these sensations into groups. And so Mill is not wholly averse to the idea " that the non-ego altogether may be but a mode in which the mind represents to itself the possible modifications of the ego." As he says in another passage,* " I do not believe that the real externality to us of anything, except other minds, is capable of proof.— The view I take of externality could not be more accurately expressed than in Professor Fraser's words : ' For ourselves we can conceive only (1) an externality to our present and transient experience in *our own* possible experience past and future, and (2) an externality to our own conscious experience in the contemporaneous, as well as in the past or future experience of *other minds.*' "

The conclusion is certainly not one with which any Idealist can disagree. The question, of course, is how far the means, by which the conclusion is reached, are satisfactory. The conclusion is one, which is in reality forced upon Mill by his predecessors in the English school, Locke, Berkeley, and Hume. But we wish to

* " Examination," p. 232, note.

know, whether, given the essential position of Sensationalism, we can from it explain all that our ordinary belief in the Existence of an External World contains.

Idealism, as I understand it, believing that all reality (and therefore the reality of the External World) is the work of Thought, proceeds to show how the mind, by "*a priori*" action, by super-imposition of forms, categories and relations, intelligibly constructs its experience into all the Order and Regularity of an External World, αὐτοῖς εἴδεσι δι'αὐτῶν τὴν μέθοδον ποιουμένη.* But Sensationalism, necessarily believing that all reality is actual sensation and its legitimate inferences, has to show how far sensations by themselves can combine, congeal, and crystallise into what we call External Facts, and thus give rise to the idea we have of an uniform Order of Nature.

Turning to Mill for guidance, we are first attracted by his mental postulates. The last of these, the Association of Ideas, we have already discussed in the preceding chapter, and the difficulty we there found was to understand how sensations can, of themselves and prompted by themselves, associate—which they must do, if the mind is to be conceived of as purely passive. The other two postulates, Expectation and Memory, Mill himself gives up, when he comes to explain " Mind." They are the " final inexplicability : " those conditions of mental action, which the theory of

* Plato, Rep. vi. s. 510.

Sensationalism cannot explain. So that, so far as the subjective postulates go, we are not much helped by the Psychological Theory.

We turn, then, to the objective postulates, or Sensations viewed in their objective aspect (for Mill's own expression " postulates in Nature " is rather misleading, inasmuch as it is the growth of the belief in Nature which we are trying to explain). They are Sensations, simultaneousness and succession of Sensations, and unions of Sensations into groups. A fourth condition of Mill which he brings in as testimony to, or verification of his process, we cannot lay much stress on here: it is our experience of what " other people do " in relation to their sensations. Of course, we do not as yet believe in other people's existence, unless we prove that there is such a thing as Externality. At all events, we cannot assume the existence of other people, and bring them in as confirmation of our own subjective processes, when we are actually tracing the growth of an Existence other than ourselves.

With regard to the other three, Sensations, of course, are their own evidence; but there is a serious gap between them and " succession," " simultaneousness " and " union into groups." The question here again is the old question—Can " relations " grow out of sensations? For that " simultaneousness," " succession " and " union into groups," are " relations," and not sensations at all, requires very little proof. Sensations are one thing: 'the links, which unite and combine them into groups, are quite another.' Now by "relations," Idealism means the "*a priori*" action of the mind, working up sensations: but Mill cannot accept such "*a priori*" action; consequently the problem becomes pressing—Can sensations in and by themselves combine and arrange themselves into "unions" and "groups"? If Association be the weird alchemy which explains such combination, well and good; but if Association itself be impossible, except to an active and synthetic self-consciousness, it cannot help us out of the difficulty.*

Such appear to me to be the difficulties of Mill's "postulates," and as the whole theory of Externality rests on the postulates, to these difficulties that theory is liable. That the conclusion is that of the Idealist needs no further assertion. If Mill's theory means anything, it certainly means that Matter is for us not something objective but merely subjective. Or, as he expressly states it, "we know no more of things than what sensations give us," and sensations testify to nothing but themselves.

That being so, we desire to ask two questions before proceeding further. In the first place, what are we to understand that knowledge, according to Mill, is? The answer, if we take these chapters we have been considering, is perfectly plain. Knowledge is the

* See note at end of Chapter.

process by which ideas are formed out of sensations, and the agreement or disagreement of these ideas would seem to be knowledge. We turn to the "Logic,"* and we find, to our amazement, that the theory that knowledge has to do with ideas is described as "one of the most fatal errors ever introduced into the philosophy of Logic." "Propositions are not assertions respecting our ideas of things, but assertions respecting the things themselves:" the doctrine that "the investigation of truth consists in contemplating and handling our ideas, or conceptions of things, instead of the things themselves" is described as "tantamount to the assertion that *the only mode of acquiring knowledge of nature is to study it at second hand, as represented in our own minds.*" What are we to make of this? The very doctrine "that the only mode of acquiring knowledge of nature is to study it at second hand, as represented in our own minds," which Mill so earnestly repudiates in his "Logic," is an exact description of the doctrine which he as earnestly maintains in "The Psychological Theory of the Belief in an External World." A better proof could hardly be furnished of the very different philosophical bases on which his two treatises respectively rest.

In the second place, we wish to know, with exactness, what Mill means by "a phenomenon"? † Does

* "Logic," bk. I. c. v. sec. 1.
† Cf. Hume, edited by Green and Grose, Introduction, vol. i. p. 168. "The juggle which the modern logic performs with the word— 'phenomenon.'"

he mean a simple intimation of a sense-perception, or does he mean a single, individual, concrete, real, fact? The first is what he ought to mean, by the requirements of his Sensationalist position. Sense gives us phenomena; with phenomena only we have to deal, in opposition to the so-called noümena, or things in themselves; a phenomenon then is a fact as it appears to us, and as it is represented by our modes of consciousness. But " phenomenon " does not mean this, when we are told, as in the " Logic," that a proposition deals with " phenomena," and that we are to study Nature first-hand, and not at second hand, as represented in our own minds. " Phenomenon " does not mean this, when the Inductive Methods are applied to phenomena to elicit their laws. Then it means a real, objective, concrete fact, and if that is immediately known by us, then we are not in the position of Idealism but of Realism.

The fact is that Mill as an Inductive Logician supposes that phenomena (objective facts) are immediately cognised by us, while Mill as a Psychologist, a critic of Hamilton, and a metaphysician, supposes that phenomena, the facts immediately cognised by us, are mere subjective presentations.

Kant, when he uses the word Phenomenon, means the product of an objective and a subjective factor, the result of a sensation on which has come the mental elation of Individuality. Mill must mean what Kant means, minus the *a priori* mental relation. But only a Realist like Hamilton can mean that a phenomenon as an objective fact, is immediately cognised,—a philosopher who believes the Sensation testifies to something beyond itself, viz., something external.*

* It is very difficult to be sure of Mill's opinions on some of the points discussed in this chapter, notwithstanding Mill's important "Appendix" in the 3rd edition. The difficulties may be briefly summarised.
 1. Are "feelings" and "sensations" equivalent expressions? Mill says as much, when he quotes with approbation James Mill's remark. "Having a sensation and having a feeling are not two things. The thing is one, the names only are two" (p. 139). But in the Appendix, Mill seems to imply more by the word "feeling": and in the Logic (Bk. i.) he says, "Feeling is a genus, of which Sensation, Emotion, and Thought are subordinate species."
 2. Do "relations" grow out of sensations by the Laws of Association in Mill's opinion? On page 13, he says, speaking of the opinions of his own school, "Place, Extension, Substance, Cause, *and the rest*, are conceptions put together out of ideas of sensation by the known laws of association." As he has just been speaking of Kantian forms, I suppose that Time and Relations generally are included in the expression "and the rest." In the Appendix, however, he takes a different tone. "We are *directly* conscious of succession, in the fact of having successive sensations" (p. 256). But in the next page he contradicts himself. "We are forced to apprehend every part of the series as linked with the other parts by something in common, *which is not the feelings themselves, any more than the succession of the feelings is the feelings themselves*" (p. 257). Are "relations" "the conditions which are themselves sensational," of which he speaks on page 249? Are they Hume's "manners of feeling," or not?
 3. The words "permanence" and "possibility" are very perplexing. "Permanent" must mean "present with every state of consciousness," and "possibility" ought to mean "idea." In that case, "matter" defined as "permanent possibility of sensation" is an explanation which sadly needs to be explained. For what is the "possible" but the "ideal"? And how then can knowledge be said to be concerned, not with "ideas," but with "things"?

CHAPTER VI.

THE PRIMARY QUALITIES OF MATTER.

"OF our sensations,"* says Mill, "there are some which we usually refer to that thread of consciousness of which they form a part, and there are others, which we are in the habit of referring to those Permanent Possibilities of Sensation, which are, in a sense, realised in them." For instance, we have the Sensations of Pleasure and Pain. These are not referred, as a general rule, to any outward object, because they are much more important to us in relation to our own consciousness. But there are other sensations, of which, as sensations, we have only a momentary consciousness: we immediately pass from them to the Permanent Possibilities of sensation, of which they are a mark. In this latter case, what we really know only as an inference is thought to be cognised directly, and Perception takes the place of Sensation. The distinction here noted, corresponds to the distinction between "the Primary" and "the Secondary" qualities of matter.

* "Examination," c. xiii. "Psychological Theory of Primary Qualities."

Having given the rationale of this historical distinction, Mill proceeds to the examination of what these Primary Qualities are. Although it is possible that we might get an idea of Matter from the sensations only of Smell, Taste, and Hearing, as a matter of fact, these sensations of Smell, Taste and Hearing are not active by themselves, but only lead to the formation of groups of Possibilities of Sensation through their connection with the sensations referable to the sense of Touch and the Muscles: in other words, these sensations are directly connected, either by laws of co-existence or causation, with the sensations which answer to the terms Resistance, Extension, and Figure. In consequence, the Possibilities of sensations of touch and the muscles, form a group within the group, an inner nucleus; and the remaining possibilities are regarded either as effects, of which this nucleus is the cause, or attributes, of which the nucleus is the substance. So our idea of Matter comes ultimately to consist of Resistance, Extension, and Figure: these are held to be its essential constituents.

Of these Primary Qualities of Matter, Resistance is the most fundamental. "Resistance" is a sensation of muscular action impeded, simultaneously with which is felt the sensation of touch. These two sensations are always felt together. We feel contact, and we know that were we to exercise our muscles, we should experience resistance. By the Law of Inseparable

Association, no sooner do we feel contact, than we cognise something external, because the former sensation is a mark of the Permanent Possibility of the sensation of resistance and muscular action. Matter, consequently, is considered a "resisting" object, because we experience simultaneously a sensation of touch (of contact) and a sensation of muscular action impeded.

More important, however, in many ways, is the account given of "Extension." The Psychological Theory of Extension derives it also from a sensation of muscular energy. It supposes a *discriminative sensibility* in muscular action, which leads the patient of the sensation to derive from the *duration* of the muscular action, the notion of Matter as an extended object, just as he derives from the *intensity* of muscular effort, the notion of Matter as a resisting object. Extension then may be construed as the sensation of a muscular effort having a certain continuance, gained by "the sweep of the arm" or "the sweep of the limb,"* and synonymous with a certain "volume of feeling." Now it is evident that this notion of Extension expresses it as a *series* of muscular efforts—a consciousness of *successive* states of muscular activity. Whence, then, the "*simultaneity*," with which we grasp the attribute of extension?

Although Mill seems to think that the simultaneity

* "Examination," pp. 269, 270.

may be transferred to it from the experience (gained previously,) of the possible simultaneity of two sensations in the mind at once, he thinks it most probable that the action of the eye contributes to the notion of Extension this idea of simultaneity. The Eye gives, in a moment of instantaneous consciousness, the notion of an extended object.* The action of the visual organ, whether in "its sweep over a wide prospect," or "its adjustment for a distant view," enables the visual sensations to stand as "symbols" for muscular and tactual sensations, which might be experienced or were actually experienced, as slowly successive. Hence it comes that our consciousness of extension is connected as an appendage with our Sensations of Sight (which, in itself, is limited to the impressions of Colour) although, in reality, derived from the sensation of continued muscular action.

Just as the sensation of continued muscular action gives the notion of linear extension, and extension in any direction, so it will also give the notion of situation and "Figure." And further, it will enable us, by the muscular sensibility connected with it, to compare different degrees of the attribute of space, *i.e.*, difference of length, surface, situation, and form. And lastly, the velocity of the motion will be also given by muscular sensibility, and we discover that a slow

* "Examination," p. 281.

motion for a long time is the same as a quicker motion with less duration.

Thus the Psychological Theory maintains that the notion of length in space, not being in our consciousness originally, is constructed out of the notion of length in time by means of muscular and tactual sensations. But the participation of the Eye in our actual notion of extension—its action taking the place, and standing as the symbol of possible, or actually-realised muscular sensations—very much alters its character, and makes us imagine that for us Extension derives its meaning from a phenomenon which is synchronous and not successive, the reverse of which, according to Mill, is really the case.

Our first task must be to see Mill's position historically, in this question of the Primary Qualities of Matter. Mill had to explain constructively, what Hume and Berkeley had done destructively. Locke's position is that, more or less, of Common-Sense. Secondary Qualities are subjective, Primary Qualities are objective. With regard to the first, we are not outside of the limits of our own consciousness; with regard to the second, we are outside, because we are able to state what are the "real" qualities of matter. Berkeley simply destroyed all difference between the two sets of qualities; a quality, like "sweetness," and a quality, like "solidity," were both equally relative to our own conscious and subjective apprehension. Hume went even farther than this: the so-called Primary were in a sense, less real than the Secondary, because more dependent on mental construction. "Solidity," for example, is more of "an idea," and therefore less "real," than a feeling to which we give the name "sweet," which is an immediate sensuous impression.

After these two philosophers, the question still remained, and required an answer—*why*, if both sets of qualities rest on the same subjective basis, is our idea of substance made up rather of qualities, like Resistance, Extension, and Figure, than of qualities like Hot, Sweet, and Cold? This is the question to which Mill had to address himself: and his answer, practically, comes to this—that sensations given in touch have more the character of *permanency*. For the rest, his reply merely is a re-affirmation of the fact: we do, as a matter of fact, connect our ideas of Externality and Matter with sensations of Touch (and afterwards, he says, of Sight) rather than with Sensations given by the other three senses, Taste, Smell, and Hearing.

What, then, are the Primary Qualities, according to Mill? Resistance, Extension, and Figure. Of these, incomparably the most important to the metaphysician is the account given of Extension. "Figure" requires no discussion, if the others are established; and "Resistance" need not occupy us long. Resistance is

THE PRIMARY QUALITIES OF MATTER. 87

gained by the sense of energy impeded, the intensity of effort giving us the notion of Matter as a Resisting Object. Of course it is obvious that mere touch, as " a surface-sense," cannot yield us these results: there can be, in mere touch, no measure of intensity of effort, or impeding of energy. These indications are the results of a sort of sixth sense, newly-invented, of which Hume was ignorant—*the Muscular Sense.**

Mere touch gives us, we are told, only " the periphery " of our bodies: the muscular sense gives us something further—resistance outside, corresponding to muscular reactions inside. Physiologically, the Muscular Sense is defined as " a Motor Nerve, under the control of the will, going out from the Brain, and moving the muscle attached to it; and of a Sensor Nerve, going back to the brain and giving intimation of the motion." Sir Charles Bell and Dr. Thomas Brown, the one a physiologist, the other a psychologist, brought into prominence the muscular sense: Mill and Bain make large use of it; in Germany, Müller, in England, Dr. Carpenter, have carried on an extensive inquiry into its nature.†

But we must not allow this account of the Muscular Sense to disconcert us, just as though we had here some means of apprehending an actuality, external to our consciousness. For of course, when we say that

* Cf. " Logic," bk. i. c. iii. s. 7, par. 3.
† McCosh, " Examination of Mill."

the Muscular Sense gives us, by means of the sense of energy impeded, the idea of Resistance, accurately interpreted, this language does not refer to any phenomena other than strictly subjective. " Sense of energy impeded " is, of course, relative to our own consciousness, just as " resistance " is strictly a feeling, and does not of itself and by itself testify to anything more. If once we have given to us, in some way, the External Object, then we see at once that the Muscular Sense may immediately acquaint us with the fact that that External Object is a resisting one : but if all that we have to start with is the Muscular Sense, as a feeling of some sort, and its intimation to us, viz., Resistance, we cannot, except with an obvious " salto mortal;" arrive at an External Object, of which this Resistance (which we only know as " feeling ") is a quality.

Possibly, too, it is right to give some weight to an objection urged by Dr. McCosh. He notices, in the account given of the action of the Muscular Sense, the part played by *volition*, which at once introduces an element above sensations. We may draw out the objection in this way. The Motor-Nerve is under the control of the Will. Now if the Will is to act, if volition determines on setting a particular member in action, we must obviously have formed some idea of the member, before we can make a volition concerning it. That is to say, before the Muscular Sense can be exerted, we must have some idea of a member, which member is, of course, external to consciousness, and yet the Muscular Sense is supposed to originate the idea of Externality.

Nor is the whole theory free, even physiologically, from doubt. That on which the inference of Externality mainly depends,—the Muscular Sense and its *discriminative sensibility* (the power, that is, which it has of distinguishing between a lesser and a greater amount of intensity of effort or impediment of energy) —has been actually denied by some physiologists.*

Sensationalist schemes of Philosophy find "Space" a difficult conception to account for: nor is this remarkable. For our conception of Space is, essentially, "synchronous," *i.e.*, we embrace together, in one and the same notion, the various parts into which Space may be and is divided. But if we rely on "sensation" and "experience," we can get to nothing more than a "succession" of parts in Space, not to that "coexistence" of parts, without which to us the conception of "Space" is meaningless. For feelings must be successive: and therefore the notion of Space which is constructed out of feeling, must be a "succession" also.

It will be interesting to observe Hume's account of "Space," † as illustrating this Sensationalistic diffi-

---

* Cf. E. H. Weber, quoted in Abbot's "Sight and Touch," who refers also to Aubert and Kammler.

† Hume's "Treatise," bk. ii. s. iii.

culty, before we turn to Mill, and his attempt to overcome it. From whence is derived the Idea of Space? Hume tells us, it is derived from eyesight. What, then, we ask, does the eyesight testify to, considered as mere feeling? Obviously, Colour. We have a feeling of colour, in the case of a table (which is Hume's illustration), a feeling of brown colour. Can it testify to anything more? Certainly not, for directly we rise from mere sensations of colour, and speak of colour, as appearing in different relations,—shaded in one part, bright in another—and go on to speak of a particular object, which is revealed to us by, or is the complex of, these relations, we are deserting the sphere of mere feeling: we have got to conceptions, to mental grouping of sensations.

Then, if extension be derived from the eyesight, and the eyesight, considered as pure feeling, testifies only to colour, is "extension" the mere feeling of colour? This will hardly be satisfactory for the mathematical sciences, which are founded on the abstract idea of space or extension, for they can hardly rest on such a meaning of extension as this. Moreover, as feelings are successive, one gone before another comes (unless they are held together by the constructive force of the mind), the only idea of space they can give rise to, is equivalent to "a sequence of sense-impressions:" in which case, the table, as interpreted by eyesight, can be only a succession of brown feelings, and not (what it should be) a co-existence of brown parts. Of course Hume's literary skill enabled him to disguise this difficulty. In the sentence, in which he discusses the growth of the idea of extension he speaks of "my senses conveying to me the impressions of *coloured points, disposed in a certain manner.*" The artifice here lurks in the italicised words.*

By what right does Hume introduce these "coloured points" — this "disposition of points in a certain manner?" Here is, at once an illegitimate, quasi-objective reference. For he cannot mean by "coloured points," mere "moments of sentient consciousness," "moments of feeling," because *these* cannot be said to be *disposed in a certain manner.* Yet, by the substitution of "coloured points, disposed in a certain manner" for "mere sensations of colour," Hume has gained exactly that co-existence and reality, which we find in our common idea of space, but which his system cannot in verity allow of.

Let us turn now to Mill's theory of the gradual formation of the Idea of Extension. Shortly put, it is this. Just as the *intensity* of muscular effort gave us the idea of Resistance or, as Mill puts it (with whatever amount of truth), the idea of matter as a resisting body: so does the *duration* of muscular effort give us the idea of Extension, or Matter as an extended object. The growth of the idea of Space can be traced as the

* Cf. Green's "Introduction to Hume," vol. i.

development of Touch-sensations, combined with a certain effort of the Muscular Sense, continued for a certain time.

Now it is worth noticing, in passing, that the Idea of Time * is pre-supposed in the account of the origin of Space. The very word " duration " of Effort has no meaning without the acknowledgment of Time, as a pre-supposed Idea. This is, of course, obvious, but it is not therefore unimportant. For Time appears to be

* With regard to "Time," and our perception thereof, Mill appears, in the main, to accept the position of Hume that the Idea of Time is merely abstracted from our experience of the succession of sensations. (Cf. "Examination," p. 247. "An entity called Time, I do not and need not postulate." Cf. what he says in the opening chapter on "the Relativity of Knowledge," and James Mill's "Analysis." Vol. ii. p. 134. "Time is a collective name for the feeling of the succession of feelings.") It is not, then, a form, or conception prior to Experience, and applied to any and every experience we obtain by an inevitable necessity arising from the mind itself : it, like everything else, is a product of Experience : and so far as the principle holds that an abstraction, as the work of thought, is less in contact with reality than the concrete "facts" from which it is obtained, the idea of Time is less real than that succession of sensations from which it is an abstraction.

If this be Mill's position (and his system as an Experimental System demands it) the criticism is pertinent which asks, whether any amount of successive sensations can give rise to the conception of a succession of sensations ? It can only in one way, if there be a mind present to each sensation, holding them in due relations to one another, and transforming into permanencies the perishing series of sense-impressions. For we can only talk of a succession, if the first of the series be in our minds equally with the last. Time, as a mental form, applied to sense, gives rise to the conception " a succession of sensations :" but the reverse hardly holds in the same way ; sensations succeeding one another cannot and do not give rise to the Idea of Time.

itself a derivative, not a primary idea. It is derived from the sequence of sense-impressions. Therefore Space is derived from that which is itself derived from sequent sensations. And so before we get to Space at all, we have to face the difficulty, how can sequent sensations give rise to the idea of Sequence itself? The difficulties of Space-derivation are dependent on the prior difficulties of Time-derivation.

Let us however pass over this point, and look narrowly at the language in which Mill and Bain describe how these Tactual and Muscular Sensations originate the idea of Extension.

The muscular sensation * "gives the feeling of linear extension, inasmuch as this is measured by the *sweep of a limb*, or other organ, moved by muscles." And again, on the next page, words meet us like "*the range of an arm*," "the total *sweep* of the arm," &c. Now here is a piece of literary artifice, not quite so clever as Hume's, because the elder philosopher was an adept at such strategy. These words "sweep" and "range" are at once intelligible, if we pre-suppose the idea of space: but what meaning are we to attach to them without such pre-supposition? What is "sweep," if not "sweep through space?" † And if these words

* "Examination," p. 269, &c.
† The argument is urged by many critics. Mill's answer in the note to the 13th chapter is, that both he and Bain have been careful to limit the expressions to "feelings." In that case, how is "space" originated at all?

are only used metaphorically, how are we one step in advance in the origination of Space, or what definite meaning can they be supposed to convey? I say nothing of the words " of the arm " in these expressions: though indeed they must mean that in some way or other, we have got hold of " the arm " as an objective reality, apart from and beyond our mere subjective consciousness. Hume talked of " points," and " disposition of points "—words which have an unmistakable objective reference, if they are to mean anything. Mill, in his turn, talks of " sweep " and " range of arm and limb," which, if they are to mean anything, must likewise involve an objective reference, viz., the pre-supposition of Space itself, as a reality.

However this may be, the Sensationalistic difficulty of constructing co-existence out of succession, still remains. The idea of Space grows somehow out of the idea of Time. Successive sensations, given by Touch and the Muscular Sense, produce ultimately the idea of Space, which is not successive—which is, in reality nothing, if it is not the co-existence of parts.

It is the merit of Mill that he sees this difficulty clearly, and that he tries to meet it. It is the Eye, he says, which converts, or seems to convert succession into co-existence.* " The conception we now have of Extension or Space is an eye-picture, and comprehends a great number of parts of Extension at once, or

* P. 275.

in a succession so rapid that our consciousness confounds it with simultaneity." Feelings of Touch are successive; then come the feelings given us by the Eye, and the result is that that which is originally known as successive, now becomes "embraced" as a co-existence.

The exact opinions of Mill with regard to the Sensations given by the Eye, are hard to be sure of. I am by no means certain that I really apprehend his meaning. What, in the case of the Eye, is immediate, intuitive, and what is derivative, inferential? Berkeley, in "the Essay on Vision," said that Colour is the immediate object of the Eye, and Distance is an inference. Mill, if we may judge from what he says in other places —as *e.g.* in his "Dissertations and Discussions" *— seems to defend Berkeley's theory of vision against his critics. So here he seems to agree that "the distinctive impressibility of the Eye is for Colour." † If that is the case, it is obvious that the Eyesight, as feeling, must give us successive sensations, in our notion of Space, just like any other Sense, and not co-existence of parts. The case is not really altered by speaking of the active or muscular sensibility of the eye. The "sweep" of the eye cannot give us, any more than the sweep of an arm, aught but successive sensations. Still the idea of co-existence of parts—the essential idea of Space—remains unaccounted for.

* Vol. ii. art. on Bailey. † P. 280.

Later speculations cut the knot by practically denying the truth of Berkeley's analysis. Müller supposes that vision at once and immediately perceives a superficies.* Thus, length and breadth, two dimensions of space, are at once perceived. It is only when we come to the perception of a Solid, that we leave the sphere of immediate intuition, and reach inferences from sensations, or a judgment. A superficies, accordingly, is immediately perceived by the eye: a solid is only mediately perceived, or reached by a judgment or inference. If Mill believed this, he could, of course, prove that co-existence of parts is given by the Eyesight: for the Eye would then immediately 'embrace' as a superficies (which is extension) that which is only successively attained by touch-sensations. But he could

---

* Rather different is Helmholtz—who disagrees with and criticises Müller. See his article on "The Recent Progress of the Theory of Vision," in the "Preussische Jahrbücher" of 1868, translated in Dr. Atkinson's "Popular Scientific Lectures of Helmholtz." In that essay, although there are many sentences, which are thoroughly in the spirit of the Berkleian analysis (*e.g.*, "It is clear that the quality of our sensations, and especially our sensations of sight, does not give us a true impression of corresponding qualities in the outer world"), the Binocular system of vision is supposed to make some difference, and (if I understand it aright) to generate our notions of distance. For the two eyes look each at different parts of the object before them. Of course, one has to learn to interpret one's signs; but the Idealist contention is that one cannot do this without the *a priori* form of Space. Once given *that*, the signs can be interpreted, the different pictures given by the two eyes being now recognised as being in different parts of Space. But only starting from one's different eye-feelings, how is the notion of Space to be gained ?

only do so by practically denying Berkeley's Theory of Vision (which he is far from doing) : and then it would surely be a work of supererogation* to trace the growth of 'Space' out of Tactual and Muscular Sensations, for to the Eye, Space would be an immediate intuition.

Here, as elsewhere, Mill would seem to halt between the Sensationalism he inherited from Hume and Berkeley, and the later speculations of the Experiential School. He acknowledges that Space, according to Tactual intimations, can only be a succession of sensations; but he seems to think that the Eyesight can grasp succession, as co-existence, which it can not do, unless it immediately perceives Space in two dimensions. If it does so perceive Space, the whole Psychological analysis is unnecessary. Space is not an inference at all, it is an Intuition.

* At least, for the present purpose. The inquiry as to the manner in which persons born blind derive " Space " from Touch, of course, remains.

CHAPTER VII.

CAUSATION AND THE UNIFORMITY OF NATURE.

AFTER our conceptions of Body and Space, and the manner in which we come to entertain them, our next concern is with the constitution of the Natural World and our belief in the processes of Nature. We have, that is to say, to examine Mill's opinions on the questions of " Causation " and " Natural Uniformity."

On what do Induction and Inductive processes depend? The ground of Induction,* answers Mill, is the Uniformity of Nature, which may be thus defined :— that what is true in certain cases is true of every other case resembling the former in certain assignable respects. How is this Uniformity of Nature proved? It is a generalisation from all our Inductions, a conclusion " per enumerationem simplicem " from inductions that we have carried out in past time.

The question naturally occurs, " Is not an 'inductio per simplicem enumerationem' a very fallacious one?"

* " Logic," bk. iii. c. iii.

It is, and it is not, answers Mill. It is in certain cases—cases of a limited range of experience. It is not in others. In the particular case we are considering, it is not fallacious for this reason: the evidence for the axiom of "Natural Uniformity" is obtained from so large a field of experience, that any real exceptions, if any such existed, must have come under our notice. These innumerable Inductions, coinciding in one result, and all pointing in one direction, cover the whole field of Nature's operations. Therefore here the "enumeratio simplex" is adequate to prove the conclusion. Or, as he says in a later chapter,* "The subject-matter of our law is so widely diffused that there is no time, place, or set of circumstances in which it is not fulfilled. It is clear, then, that the law can not be frustrated by any counteracting causes, except such as never occur, and cannot depend upon any collocations except such as exist at all times and places." Further, of those phenomena of which we do not positively know it to be true, one after another is constantly passing from this class into that of known examples of its truth, and any deficiency, or absence of positive knowledge of its truth, may always be accounted for by the variety and obscurity of the phenomena in these special cases.

At the same time, Mill adds, we cannot extend the validity of this Law of Causation beyond the limits of

* "Logic," bk. iii. c. xxi. vol. ii.

our Experience: we cannot say that every event follows from a cause in distant stellar worlds, for example: such an extension is unauthorised and illegitimate.*

Another difficulty occurs. If Induction itself rests for its validity on the Uniformity of Nature (as its major premiss), and the Uniformity of Nature rests on a number of Inductions, are we not here in a vicious circle of inference? The answer, says Mill, lies in a proper view of the function of the Major Premiss in a Syllogism. If we suppose that the conclusion really rests on, and is proved by, the Major Premiss, then obviously we cannot but suppose that the circular form of the reasoning given above, is fatal to its validity. But such is not the function of the Major Premiss. It is but the summary, the record, the memorandum in concise language of our experience, so far as it has gone. Both the conclusion, therefore, and the major premiss are alike conclusions from the antecedently observed particular cases. Hence, both the conclusion reached by Induction, and the major premiss—the Uniformity of Nature—are proved by the instances we have observed before, *i.e.*, by our experience.†

After these statements of the absolute validity of the Uniformity of Nature, we proceed to Causation,

* "Logic," bk. iii. c. xxi. s. 4. last par.
† Ibid., bk. iii. c. iii. s. 1 ; c. xxi. s. 4.

and the definition of a "Cause."* "The notion, of Cause, being the root of the whole theory of Induction, it is indispensable," says Mill, "that this idea should, with the utmost practicable degree of precision, be fixed and determined." Now the Law of Causation is this: (1) That every phenomenon, which has a beginning, must have some Cause, and (2) That given the Cause, the effect will invariably follow (*minus* counteracting causes). What, then, is a Cause? It is an antecedent, and further, it is an *invariable* antecedent. But we must not suppose that "cause" is necessarily one single phenomenon: it is, most frequently, an assemblage of phenomena, the effect following upon a sum of several antecedents. We may, it is true, draw a distinction between a Cause, and the Conditions or the Occasion, the Cause being, as it were, the last in order of time, immediately following on which occurs the event; but this is a convenient, more than a logical distinction. The Cause is the sum of conditions: the sum, in fact, of positive and negative conditions ("positive" being "the conditions which must be present," "negative" being "those which must be absent"). These negative conditions are further specified as being, either "Counteracting Causes" (which neutralise the effect of the other antecedents by producing their own) or "Preventing Causes" (which destroy the effect, by simply arresting it).

* "Logic," bk. iii. c. v. s. 2.

So far then, Cause is defined as "the invariable antecedent, or antecedents." Is this all that there is in our idea of Cause? No, for day is the invariable antecedent of night (and vice versâ), and yet no one calls day the cause of night. Why is this? Because the sequence of night upon day depends upon another condition—viz., the rotation of the earth and the consequent absence of the sun. The cause then, must be "unconditional": it must produce the effect, under any imaginable supposition with regard to other things. If night followed day, whether the rotation of the earth ceased or not, then day might rightly be called the cause of night. But it does not, therefore it is not the cause. The Cause, then, is the invariable, unconditional antecedent. "The Cause is the antecedent, or concurrence of antecedents, on which the effect is invariably and unconditionally consequent." *

Some further questions, relative to this general subject, are discussed by Mill, which we may briefly summarise.

Is the distinction between "agent" and "patient" a real one? No, it is merely verbal, patients are always agents. A man's condition, when he takes prussic acid, is as much the cause, or agent of his death, as the prussic acid.†

Must a cause always precede, by ever so short an

---

* "Logic," bk. iii. c. v. s. 6. † Ibid. s. 4.

interval, its effect? No, Mill seems to answer; sometimes it is simultaneous.*

Is the type of Causation, and the only source from which we derive the idea, our own voluntary agency? Certainly not. For the idea of "Power" cannot be derived from my will producing my bodily motions, from Mind acting on Body, because Mind only acts on Body *mediately*, through a chain of antecedents and consequents (our nerves and muscles) of which we are not conscious. Nor yet can it be said that the Idea of Power comes from the power of Self over the volitions, "from myself, producing my Will," because Mill professes that so far as he is concerned, he is not conscious of this power at all. The fact is that the notion of "productive power" as applied to causation, is merely a delusion: all that experience does or can generate is an idea of invariable sequence.†

It is not difficult to find difficulties in Mill's account of Causation, for Mill himself, with that frank inconsistency, with which many of his theories are expounded, has taken care to leave them on the surface.

The first difficulty is concerned with the relation which he exhibits between the Law of Causation and

* "Logic," bk. iii. c. v. s. 7.
† Mill's "Examination of Hamilton," c. xvi. pp. 356–361. Cp. "Logic," bk. iii. c. v. s. 11.

the Law of the Uniformity of Nature. They are, of course, not the same thing. The first means that nothing happens without a cause of some sort, the second that the whole physical world exhibits uniform methods and laws. The first means that we are compelled to believe that every antecedent has a consequent, and every consequent an antecedent, the second that we are compelled to believe that uniform sequences of events and causes hold in every possible department of our knowledge about Nature.

What is the relation between these two? Evidently this—that from the first—viz., that there is a regular succession in phenomena—we arrive at the second— that all nature exhibits uniform laws. But in all extensions of our knowledge of physical and other phenomena, how do we proceed? We assume that, if we look long enough, the event we are inspecting will be proved to have a cause, because all nature is uniform. Thus the ground of a fresh Induction is that which is itself the last result of an Induction. We may press the difficulty even a little farther. It is obvious that until we have exhausted all the different departments of knowledge about Nature, we cannot be perfectly sure that the Law of Causation holds everywhere. It must be therefore dangerous to bring in the assumption of uniformity to fortify ourselves in reducing fresh investigations into cases of this law of uniformity.

Mill's answer to this is that, in reality, the conclusion of our syllogisms about Nature is proved along with the assumed major premiss by the amount of cases we have observed before. That is to say that experience proves concurrently *both* the increasing validity of the General Law of Uniformity *and* the particular instance we are at present observing. Such a conclusion, then, depends strictly on the Experience gone through, and both General Law and Particular Fact are valid exactly to the same extent—viz., so far as they are inferences from past experience. This is all the necessity and universality of the Law, that any " inductio per simplicem enumerationem " can possibly attain to.

The difficulty with regard to this circular argument —that Induction depends on the Law of Uniformity and Uniformity itself depends on Induction—has been met in other ways, and some of them appear certainly more satisfactory than Mill's avowal, which makes our belief in Uniformity depend on our past experience.

The later Experiential School would meet it, I suppose, in this way. It is true that in fresh cases of Induction, the Uniformity of Nature, as a Law, is logically prior to this or that uniformity which we prove by its means. But though logically prior, it yet may be historically posterior. Logically, a postulate, it yet may be, historically, a product. In other words, men start *now* in their fresh explorations with the belief in Uniformity, but the belief itself is the slow result of accumulated experiences in past generations. Prior to the Individual, it is posterior to the Race, just like those notions of Time and Space, which men begin with now, as *a priori* notions, though in reality they are (according to Mr. Herbert Spencer*) the products of their fathers' *a posteriori* experience. The same discrimination between logical priority and historical posteriority serves also to explain other notions. Thus, for example, logically, the Universal is prior to the Particular: historically, the Particular is prior to the Universal. Logically, Duty, as an idea, is prior to particular cases of "what ought to be done:" historically, we arrive at our idea of Duty after a series of particular dutiful acts.

But this explanation is due to that enlargement of the sphere of Experience, which we have as 'the note' of more modern experientialists than Mill. Experience, to them, is not experience of the individual, but experience of the race: and so many of these difficulties (among others the proof of the validity of Geometrical axioms) are met. But in Mill, with his use of "simplex enumeratio" all we have is a belief in Uniformity seemingly proportionate to the experience which *we*, not our forefathers, have undergone. However capable of extension the theory may be, as a matter of fact, by Mill it is not so extended.

* H. Spencer's "First Principles," pp. 162—165. "Psychology," vol. i., pp. 466—468.

The other method of explanation is "the Simple Intuitionist Method," as Mill calls it, which he expressly rejects. In its best expression, it is this :— that Causation, Causality, is a mental category, with which we start to make our experience of Nature intelligible for us. It cannot be intelligible, unless it is reduced to order. Experience, as furnished by sequent sensations, is a chaos. Only Thought can produce Order by the superimposition of forms, relations, categories. Only Thought can produce therefore (in the only sense in which the word is capable of any meaning) "Reality." Causation being, then, a category, a form, with which we start—prior to experience, and not given by experience,—it is as clear as daylight why the ground of Induction is the belief in Universal Causation. We reduce our fresh experiences to order simply by bringing upon them the category of Causality.

From this point of view, all Mill's instances to prove that the belief in Uniformity has grown to be what it is, and was not believed in originally, are so many fresh proofs of the originality of our form of Causality. Τύχη, τὸ αὐτόματον, and the rest of them, were so many provisional explanations of Causation, awaiting further experience. The whole content of our form of Causality was not yet complete; and in the absence of such full content, (only to be gained by experience) the explanations of the Greek philosophers are to us inadequate, though they were to them possibly quite adequate from the point of view of their incomplete experience. The form was there, as a δύναμις, waiting for content, waiting for experience, waiting to become ἐντελέχεια. The very age of Mythology gives the best illustration of how natural it is for men to apply categories of Causation. The Greeks, in a Mythological age, were anxious to provide causes for everything,—causes for the wind, in an Æolus, causes for thunder in Hephæstos, causes for sea-storms, in Poseidon. They did not realise, it is true, the Uniformity of Nature,—that all Nature exhibits uniform processes of action and abjures theories of Occasionalism; they simply could not: they had not had the experience. But they strictly believed that every event has a cause of some sort, however fancifully the category of Causation was applied. Still less, of course, can it be urged that Human Volition forms any exception to this process. Mill himself notes that some Intuitionists believe that the relation of the Will or Ego to action, forms the type of all Causation. And naturally so; for men, in their application of the category of Causality, are guided by those phenomena, of which they have earliest experience. That some philosophers do not believe in " the uniformity of Nature" as applied to the sphere of human volition, does not in any way affect the question of the originality of the form of Causation. Whether they do or do not believe that a motive stands to an act, in precisely the same relation as a physical antecedent stands to a physical consequent, they do not, therefore, believe that human action is uncaused: the Ego, the Self is the Cause,—a free cause, a first cause.

Leaving now the relation between Causation as a Law and the belief in the Uniformity of Nature, let us proceed to Mill's definition of Cause. Here we had better put aside all collateral issues, and confine ourselves to the main point.*

What is a Cause? It is an invariable unconditional Antecedent. Let us take each of these attributes in turn.

The relation of Cause and Effect, of Antecedent and Consequent, is discovered by Experience, and yet Cause is the invariable antecedent.

Does not this word "invariable" open the whole difficulty again? for what does "invariable" in com-

---

* Difficulties there undoubtedly are in some of Mill's subsidiary remarks. *E.g.* The cause precedes the event, says Mill, sometimes, and yet the distinction between Agent and Patient, is utterly unreal, the Patient is always an Agent. If so it would obviously be truer to say, the Cause never precedes the Effect, for the Effect (being the Patient) is always a Cause (Agent) and therefore can never be posterior to it. Or again, it is not true, according to Mill, to say "cessante causâ cessat et effectus," for a body through which a sword has passed, continues dead, even when the sword has been removed. That is to say, the patient continues, the agent is removed. Yet Patients are always Agents. The Body must be conceived of as continuously the Cause of its own death—a somewhat unnecessary inversion of ordinary language.

mon parlance mean? That to which no exception has been or can be discovered. The last part—the words "can be" are as important as the first. But what must "invariable" mean to Mill? That to which no exception *has been* discovered. In other words "invariability" is exactly measured by the amount of experience undergone. It is a parallel use to the word "inconceivability." "Inconceivability," for Mill, is strictly relative to experience; so too is invariability. It can have no other meaning.

The misfortune is that Mill is supposed to be in advance of Hume, because he is more scientific. Which is the more logical here? Hume said that Experience of antecedents and consequents led to the formation of a custom of expecting the consequent when we found the antecedent. Mill says that the Cause is the antecedent, invariable so far as our experience has gone. The difference between the custom (founded on past experiences) of finding a consequent, when we come across an antecedent, and Mill's assertion that Cause is the antecedent, invariable, so far as our experience has gone, is certainly not very great. If there is any difference, it is that Hume confines himself within what his system allows him, while Mill, in using the word invariable, does not always explain that he only means "unvaried." As to any real objective validity in Causality, it must be denied by one just as much as by the other. Hume openly denies it. Mill does so quite as much when he makes the relation depend upon a number of experiences, which are of course subjective. If it expresses more than this, if it is an objective relation between objective facts, we at once want to know, how Mill's account of externality, limiting it to Permanent Possibilities of Sensation, can admit either of such an objective relation, or of such objective facts, between which the relation is to hold.

Let us turn to Mill's second adjective, the word "unconditional." I suppose that there is no student of Mill who has not felt some difficulty in understanding how this attribute of "unconditionality" is meant to be applied and used. We are told that the cause is the sum of "the conditions," antecedent to an event: * and yet we are told that the cause is "unconditional." † We are told that an effect only follows a cause in the absence of counteracting phenomena: and yet that if the cause is real, the effect follows "under any imaginable supposition with regard to other things." ‡ Mill's instance of the relation of Night and Day does not throw much light on our confusion. Day is not the cause of night, says Mill, because Night following on Day depends on another condition—viz., the rotation of the earth. But inasmuch as it would appear that the precedence of day is one of the conditions (for it is implied in the rotation of the earth), the theory

* "Logic," bk. iii. c. v. s. 3.   † Ibid., s. 6.   ‡ Ibid., s. 6, par. 2.

which makes a Cause the sum of conditions, must include that precedence, in the cause of night. And indeed it is difficult to conceive why the analysis which resolves Causation into observed sequence, should refuse to find in Day the cause of Night. The spirit, at all events, of Hume's discussion seems to find it quite a satisfactory enough instance to give of the relation of Causation.*

The word "unconditional," in reality, rests on a view of the relation of mind to nature, quite different from that which Mill unfolds in his Psychological theories. Starting from a purely subjective basis of feeling, it is hard, indeed, to understand its meaning: but if we start from any realistic theory, it becomes, of course, intelligible enough. From Mill, at all events, we are entitled to demand this much: that either he should refuse to speak of Cause as the sum of conditions, or else refuse to define Cause, as the unconditional *antecedent*. He must either draw a clear distinction between Cause and Condition (which he does not do) or else abandon his adjective "unconditional."

We see, perhaps, the difficulty more clearly, when we observe how Mill has to limit his "unconditionality." "Unconditional" just like "invariable" means only "so far as experience has gone." Therefore, although "unconditional" is defined as "under any imaginable supposition with regard to other things," we find that

* "Inquiry," s. 4, p. 1.

the latter words only mean under any supposition with regard to the things, which have come under our experience. Thus in distant parts of the stellar regions, events may well be imagined to follow without a cause, just as in that nebulous region $2+2$ may $=5$.* That is to say that intelligence coming across new phenomena may have to alter its laws. No clearer proof is needed to show how little the words "invariable" and "unconditional" mean. We surely ought to mean by them that they hold good for all intelligence: that even if we do arrive at the study of phenomena in distant stellar regions, there too we shall apply our category of Causation just as much as we do in regions that have come already under our study. Then "invariable" means what it implies. But with Mill, it only means "unvaried within the limits of our experience," not absolutely invariable.

The conclusion is forced upon us that these words, "invariable" and "unconditional," by which Mill "developes" his predecessor's doctrine, are but the darkening of the clear counsels of Hume. Hume we could understand: but then Hume invalidated Science. Mill, to save Science, adds fresh words. The relation of Cause and Effect is still merely a subjective association, based on past sensations, past experience: yet the relation must be conceived as "invariable" and "unconditional." Hence, complexity and confusion of spirit.

* "Logic," bk. iii. c. xxi, s. 4, last par.

One word, finally, as to the opinion, combated by Mill, both in the "Logic," Bk. iii. c. v. and the chapter on Sir W. Hamilton—the opinion, viz., that Volition is the source and type of all our ideas of Power, and therefore, of Causation. Mill asks, What Idea of Power do we find in ourselves? (much the same question as Hume asked). Is it Power to act, or Power to will? If the former, there are so many steps between the originating impulse and the consequent action—so much intermediate action of muscles, &c., of which we are ignorant,—that no idea of Power can thence be derived.

This does not appear a wholly satisfactory criticism. A despot, I imagine, feels a real power in giving his orders, though he may be ignorant of the various officials through whom his orders get executed, if he is sure that they will be executed somehow. Some such assurance certainly is possessed by the Will.

The second alternative—that what we feel is a Power of Self over the Volitions, or a Power to Will, Mill disposes of without argument. Mill, "in common with one-half the psychological world," is wholly unconscious of having any such power. It does not necessarily follow that the other half of the psychological world is equally unconscious. The argument, if argument it be, is capable of too easy a retort.

But in reality, the opinion itself, that finds in Self and in Volition the type of Power in Causation, is found, I need scarcely say, in Mansel and others and not in Kant. Mansel says * (following in the steps of Cousin, to whom he is largely indebted), that the soul is *a power conscious of itself.* To Kant, any such assertion would hardly commend itself. To say this of the Soul, is to rise above Categories, is to treat the Soul as a Noumenon, and not, as we can only know it, to treat it as exhibiting Phenomena. In one sense, of course, the mere fact of *a priori* mental Categories assumes a certain power in the " pure Ego " to impose them; the mere fact of its bringing a Category of Causation to bear in the construction of an Intelligible World, implies a certain mental activity. But Kant denied the Power of the individual Self over Volition and Actions, and in that sense denied Free Will to the Ego. On the other hand, Free Will, as shown in Morality, is brought back again. But we are only concerned with the Logical aspect of this question, and from that point of view, such a notion of Power in the Self, is alien to the critical methods of Kant.

* " Prolegomena Logica." p. 139.

CHAPTER VIII.

MATHEMATICAL AXIOMS AND NECESSARY TRUTHS.

WE proceed to the foundations of Geometry and Arithmetic, or in other words to Mill's treatment of Necessary Truths.

A passage in Mill's Autobiography which has been recently quoted,* shows that with regard to these Necessary Truths, Mill purposely chose for his consideration Mathematical Axioms, because thus he thought he should carry the war into the very citadel of the enemy. If the Axioms of Geometry were shown to be inductions from experience, much more would other so-called necessary truths, cease to be considered "*a priori.*"

To this attempt, then—to make Mathematical Axioms the result of Experience,—Mill devotes himself in " Logic," Bk. II. c. v. and vi.

These chapters may be divided into three separate questions.

* By Professor Jevons, in *Contemporary Review* for December, 1877.

MATHEMATICAL AXIOMS.

(i.) What is the meaning of Necessary Truth?

(ii.) In what sense and to what extent are Mathematical Truths necessary? or in other words—what is the meaning of Mill's "Hypothetical Mathematics?"

(iii.) Are Axioms Experimental Truths?

(i.) Necessary truth as ordinarily defined, is supposed to be that which is independent of any and every experience. It is *a priori* truth.

Such is, however, not the sense of Necessary Truth o Mill. Necessity to him is necessity and certainty of Inference—not certainty or necessity of truth. In other words the term is applicable to the process of reasoning, not to the *a priori* conditions of reasoning. ("The certainty ascribed is nothing whatever but certainty of inference.") But inference from what? Inference from assumptions, which, by the conditions of the enquiry are not to be questioned. This then is Mill's definition of Necessary Truth, "Necessary Truth is such as necessarily follows from assumptions which cannot be questioned." Why these assumptions are not to be questioned, is a query to which we shall return later.

(ii.) "The character of necessity, ascribed to the truths of Mathematics,* and even the peculiar certainty (sometimes) attributed to them is an illusion," says Mill. Why? Because they relate to purely imaginary objects. "There does not exist either in nature, or

* Mill's "Logic," Bk. ii. c. 5, sec. 1.

in the human mind any objects exactly corresponding to the definitions of Geometry." There is no such thing as a "point without magnitude" or a "straight line,—length without breadth," or a perfect circle. Therefore the assumption implied in the definitions of Geometry "that there exist real things conformable to the definitions" is false.*

Now the conclusions of Geometry follow from the definitions, and the definitions themselves are built upon the hypothesis that there exist real things conformable thereto. Therefore Geometry rests upon a hypothesis—or in other words it is concerned not with such points, circles, straight lines, as are seen in nature; but with ideal points, ideal circles, &c.

The same thing holds good also of the science of number.† "In all propositions concerning numbers, a condition is implied without which none of them would be true, and that condition is an assumption which may be false. The condition is that $1 = 1$, that all the numbers are numbers of the same or of equal units. Let this be doubtful, and not one of the propositions of Arithmetic will hold true." Arithmetic then, and the Science of Numbers as well as Geometry, rest on a hypothesis, an assumption.

What is the conclusion? It is stated very clearly by Mill. ‡ Mathematics, of course, is the type of a

---

* "Not strictly true," ninth edition.
† "Logic," bk. ii. c. vi., sec. 3.   ‡ Ibid., sec. 4.

Deductive Science, and its method rests on hypotheses. The result is in Mill's language "that the Method of all Deductive Sciences is hypothetical." "They proceed by tracing the consequences of certain assumptions, leaving for separate consideration whether the assumptions are true or not, and if not exactly true, whether they are a sufficiently near approximation to the truth."

While elaborating his own view, Mill takes occasion to adduce arguments against another view of Mathematical Necessity, viz., that of the Nominalists, who would resolve all such necessary Truths into merely analytical propositions.* According to them (and we may remember that Hobbes and Leibnitz are among them) the Definitions and Theorems of the Science of Number are merely verbal. We are analysing what we mean by particular terms, straight lines or units, &c., and we affirm no more in the predicate when we say that two and one are three, than what we have already implicitly affirmed in the subject. The view is supported by the argument that we do not carry ideas of any particular thing along with us, when we manipulate algebraical or arithmetical symbols, as a and x. In answer to this, Mill asserts that we are throughout dealing with things and not with symbols. "Ten must mean ten bodies, or ten sounds, or ten beatings of the pulse." The Symbols are things, and our operations

* "Logic," chap. vi. sec. 2.

upon them express facts. As to the other argument of the Nominalists that the Propositions of Number, when considered as Propositions relating to things, all seem to be identical propositions, Mill replies that though the subject and predicate of a numerical proposition may have the same denotation (denoting the same objects) yet they may have a different connotation (as implying different states of those same objects). In "two and one = three," for instance, the subject says this "▫ ▫ and ▫," the predicate this "▫▫▫."

(iii.) We come now to the third point—that *Axioms are experimental truths.** "What is the ground for our belief in axioms—what is the evidence on which they rest? They are experimental truths: generalizations from observation." The evidence upon which we believe them is of the same kind as the evidence upon which we believe any other fact of external nature— our *experience* of their truth. They are the simplest and easiest cases of generalization from experience.

In order to support this view, Mill has to undertake two tasks.

i. He has to show that the evidence derived from experience is sufficient to prove axioms.

This he does by pointing out how experience confirms them every moment in our lives. Experimental proofs crowd upon us in profusion without any instance

* "Logic," chap. v. sec. 4.

MATHEMATICAL AXIOMS.

of a possible exception. If then experience is sufficient to convince us of their truth, why should we be at the pains of supposing other "*a priori*" evidence necessary?

ii. In the next place, he has to defend his theory against attacks.

(*a.*) "Axioms are seen to be true by merely *thinking* of them, not by actual experiment of seeing and feeling." But, says Mill, Imagination can so reproduce sensations of form that our *mental pictures* of lines, circles, &c., are as fit subjects for experimentation, as the realities.

(*β.*) "The axioms contain an assertion of invariability and universality, *e.g.*, one axiom says, two straight lines cannot meet if prolonged to infinity. How is this to be explained by an experience which can never talk of an *infinite* distance?" Mill answers: that we know that, if the two straight lines would meet, they would meet at a finite distance, and we can in imagination transport ourselves to that point, and there in imagination discover that the two convergent lines are not straight lines, but crooked ones. Imagination, and its power to reproduce sensations of form, help us over this difficulty.

(*γ.*) "But the contradictory of these axiomatic truths is *inconceivable.*" Mill replies, that what is inconceivable is neither necessarily, nor always false. For inconceivability is altogether an accidental thing, or as

Mill puts it, " Both what persons can and what they cannot conceive is very much an affair of accident, and depends altogether on their experience and their habits of thought." If we have in past experience frequently and constantly found a Proposition true, we believe its contradictory to be inconceivable. If, on the contrary, we have ever found it false, or if there exist analogies which suggest the possibility of its ever being false, then its contradictory becomes conceivable.

Moreover, we have several examples of Propositions once regarded as inconceivable, now recognised not merely as conceivable but as being the only true accounts.* E.g., to Newton, that a body should act where it is not, was inconceivable; now it is recognised, says Mill, in the theory of Gravitation and Magnetism. And on the other hand, we have instances of truths really arrived at by long experience and investigation, which have become so familiar, that some scientific men hold them to be necessary truths, e.g., the first law of motion (which by some is held to be a necessary truth), and the laws of chemical composition.

So the test of inconceivableness proves nothing, except that " two ideas are so firmly associated in our minds that we find it impossible to disconnect them."

Hence the general result follows—that axioms are experimental truths.

* " Logic," bk. ii. c. v, sec. 6.

In examining Mill's doctrines on the subject of Mathematics and Necessary Truths, there are two parts of the subject which we had better keep distinct. The first is expressed in the question:

> (1.) How far is Mill's own account of Mathematics and Geometry satisfactory and consistent with itself?

The second will run thus:

> (2.) Can we believe that Necessity and Universality are to be gained by the Association of Ideas, or, to put it differently, does Mill satisfactorily dispose of the test of Inconceivability of the opposite?

I. Let us first clearly see the difference between Mill and Hume in respect of Mathematical truths.

With Hume,* all lines, angles, triangles, and figures with which the Geometrician is conversant, were nothing other than those which we have come across in our experience. Consequently Hume can only allow the mathematician an indefinite approach to exactness. It is all very well for the mathematician to pronounce all right angles equal, but any perfect equality—an equality "beyond what we have instruments and art to ascertain,"—Hume says is "a mere fiction of the mind, useless as well as incomprehensible." From the progressive correction of our actual measurements we have a *tendency to feign* perfect exactness, perfect

* Hume's "Treatise," part ii. sec. 4.

equality in these cases, but it is nothing else than a fiction. In perfect consistency with this we find Hume denying the infinite divisibility of extension. And throughout Hume's spirit is the same, as indeed it must be for any philosopher, who makes all truths (and therefore all Mathematical truths) rest on experience.

But just as Hume's doctrine of Cause was supposed to invalidate the possibility or truth of Natural Science, so too Hume's doctrine of Mathematical truth evidently supposes " an exactness " very different from what the mathematician himself assumes. And just as Mill made some additions to Hume's doctrine of Causation to save Physics, so too he adds to his predecessor's doctrine of Geometry to save Mathematical Science. The addition is this : that mathematical deductions depend on a hypothesis. We suppose, according to Mill, figures exactly corresponding to our definitions, though such do not really exist. The definitions, in fact, represent ideas, though not ideas to which real objects can be found exactly answering. The lines, angles, and figures are ideal lines, angles, and figures. With Hume, on the contrary, all ideas were merely copies of impressions, and therefore our idea of a line could only be a copy of our impression of a line.

This hypothetical character of Mathematics Mill derived from Dugald Stewart, and it is a refinement on Hume. Is this refinement an improvement?

It is and it is not. We welcome with satisfaction the admission that there can be in the mind ideas, which are not copies of sensible things—ideas to which no external counterpart can exactly be found. We are glad to learn that the mind can manipulate ideal figures, and reason about them, and draw deductions from them —quite apart from the external (so-called) realities, with which we are conversant in experience.

But then, what becomes of the assertion in the "Logic," that the theory "that knowledge consists in the agreement or disagreement of ideas, is the most fatal mistake that ever retarded a scientific observer"? Knowledge deals with things, not with our ideas of things, says Mill. But Mathematical Knowledge, at all events, seems to deal with our ideas of things, and not with things,—with our ideas of straight lines, and not with straight lines, such as we meet with in experience. It is perhaps a little superfluous of Mill to say that ten means ten things, ten beats of the pulse, ten counters, &c., after this admission.

And further, what have we heard of the mind hitherto, in Mill's system, which will account for this idealising power? The mind is only the permanent possibility of undergoing sensations. Sensations, and associations of sensations and ideas, give us the sum total of our mental furniture on the intellectual side. How then can the mind give us ideal lines, such as do not correspond with what Mill calls external realities?

How can it have ideas to which no external objects can be found answering? Of course Mill treats the idealising power as an illusion. But just as Hume might be called upon to account for his "tendency to feign," of which he makes such conspicuous use, so Mill may be called upon to account for this idealising power, this power of framing hypothetical straight lines, which he uses in accounting for mathematical truth.

The real difficulty emerges later. The difficulty is to bring into harmony this hypothetical character of definitions, and the other doctrine that axioms are nothing but experimental truths. For if "two straight lines cannot enclose a space" be a truth known only by experience, when we talk about straight lines we can only mean such straight lines as are known in experience. If, on the other hand, the straight lines we talk about, are not straight lines known in experience, but ideal straight lines, the axiom in question cannot be learnt from experience, because experience never testifies to it, never presenting us with lines really straight.

Either, then, the ideal straight line must be an exact copy of a real straight line, or else axioms are not founded on Experience. Which is Mill's opinion? It is impossible to say. Is our mental image an exact copy of a reality, or is it not? In the first section of chapter v. he says, "There exist no points without magnitude; no lines without breadth, nor perfectly straight; no circles with all their radii exactly equal, nor squares with all their angles perfectly right. Their existence, so far as we can form any judgment, would seem to be inconsistent with the physical constitution of our planet at least, if not of the universe." In the fifth section he says, " The imaginary lines exactly resemble real ones," and again, " We can frame a mental image, which we may rely on as being precisely similar to the reality."*

II. We proceed to Mill's treatment of the test of Inconceivability.

The question now is this: Are the recognised tests of such Truths as the first truths of Mathematics (and indeed all truths of the same stringency)—viz., Necessity and Universality, sufficiently accounted for by the laws of Association? The easiest mode of approaching this question is to look at that test which is the negative form of terms like " Necessity " and " Uni-

---

* I need not enlarge on this point, as it was strenuously insisted on by Professor Stanley Jevons in his article in the *Contemporary Review* for December, 1877. His summing up of Mill's position is clear, and is adequately supported by his references.
    1. Perfectly straight lines do not really exist.
    2. We experiment upon imaginary straight lines.
    3. These imaginary straight lines exactly resemble the real ones.
    4. If these imaginary straight lines are not perfectly straight, they will not enable us to prove the truths of Geometry.
    5. If they are perfectly straight, then the real ones which exactly resemble them must be perfectly straight, ergo, perfectly straight lines do exist.

versality"—viz., "the Inconceivability of the Opposite Assumption." The first truths of Mathematics are Necessary and Universal, because the opposite assumption is inconceivable, because we cannot even conceive the possibility of straight lines ever enclosing a space.

Mill says that Inconceivability is an accidental thing, depending on experience, and association of ideas.* Inconceivability is of course an ambiguous term, and before we can assent to this, we have to see in what senses it is capable of being used. Fortunately Mill himself helps us here. In his chapter on "The Philosophy of the Conditioned" in "The Examination of Hamilton" he distinguishes three senses of the word.

Inconceivable means—

(α) that of which the mind can form no representation, either because no attributes are given out of which a representation could be framed, or because the attributes given are incompatible.

(β) that of which, though the mind can form a representation, it cannot conceive a realisation. In this sense the mind is, by the law of association, temporarily debarred from believing it.

(γ) that, which the mind cannot construe to itself, through a higher notion, or conceive as the

* "Logic," bk. iii. c. v. s. 9.

consequent of a certain reason. This is a Hamiltonian sense of the word, which would render all first truths inconceivable, and must therefore be rejected.*

If a thing, continues Mill, is inconceivable in the third sense, it can, obviously, be believed with full understanding. If it is inconceivable in the second sense, it can yet be believed, because we can represent it to ourselves, and "the inability to conceive" only rests upon a limited experience. If it is inconceivable in the first sense,

> (*a*) if we can attach any meaning to it, it may be believed, but without understanding, *i.e.*, it may be believed, because if false it would contradict something which is otherwise known to be true, or it may be taken on Authority; but
>
> (*b*) if we cannot attach any meaning to it at all, belief is impossible.

Now, in which of these senses, is it inconceivable that two straight lines should enclose a space? Evidently in the first sense, the attributes given are incompatible—straightness does not accord with the enclosure of space. In the second sense of the term, the Antipodes were inconceivable to our forefathers. They could indeed form a picture of them, but they were debarred from believing in them because all ex-

* "Examination," pp. 83-89.

perience hitherto had pointed in an opposite direction. Here possibly the association of Ideas generated by experience is quite adequate to explain the inconceivability. Is it sufficient to explain inconceivability in the first sense, where inconceivable=unpicturable; or where, in other words, it seems to go clean against the forms of the thinking mind itself? Mill says it is.* "We cannot conceive two straight lines as enclosing a space, because enclosing a space means approaching and meeting a second time; and the mental image of two straight lines which have once met, is inseparably associated with the representation of them as diverging." And again,† "We should probably have no difficulty in putting together the two ideas supposed to be incompatible, if our experience had not first inseparably associated one of them with the contradictory of the other."

This is, of course, simply an assertion, not even adequately supported by instances, for the instances come mainly from the second sense of the term inconceivable. It is therefore certainly incumbent upon us to examine it somewhat further.

In the first place, it is to be noticed, that not only is the common consciousness of mankind opposed to such a travesty of the terms "necessity," "universality," "inconceivability of the opposite," but also philosophers. Leibnitz and Hobbes, for instance, despairing

* "Examination," p. 85.   † Ibid. p. 85.

of getting "necessity" and "universality" out of a synthesis of experiences, attempt to get them out of an analysis of consciousness. According to this theory, the axioms (and all Necessary Truth), are merely Analytic judgments, we are merely analysing what we mean by the name. But Mill expressly rejects this view. With him, Axioms are synthetic, *i.e.*, more is expressed in the predicate than is stated in the subject, and yet, propositions which add to our knowledge (synthetic) attain to universality and necessity by adding experience to experience.

Kant simply falls back on these tests, as all sufficient; where we have synthetic judgments, as these axioms are, and yet judgments which are necessary and universal, there we may be sure, according to Kant, of "a priori" action of the mind.

Even Herbert Spencer* opposes Mill on this point. With him, the inconceivability of the contradictory is the ultimate basis of all beliefs. It is the universal postulate. "Whenever the contradictory of a Proposition is inconceivable, that Proposition must be accepted as true." Being then the final ground of all our beliefs, intuitive as well as inferential, it must be that of axioms among the rest.

Let us approach this question from another side.

---

* H. Spencer's "Psychology," vol. ii., p. 406 and following. So too G. H. Lewes, "History of Philosophy," Introduction "The Test of Truth."

According to Mill, the necessity and universality of axioms are due to an inseparable association of ideas in experience. Evidently, unless the Association is inseparable, Experience cannot generate universality and necessity. Now, does experience testify to the truth of these axioms so constantly as to be able to produce inseparable associations? Why they are contradicted, so far as experience goes, constantly, and as a frequent matter of observation. " Every child who looks down a long street, sees two parallel right lines converging. Every one who puts a straight rule into water, may observe that a crooked line is the shortest way between two points (its extremities)."* What is the mental process in such cases? We believe in our axioms even when experience contradicts them,—as against and in the teeth of experience. Mill's own illustration of railway lines which seem to meet is an instance in point.

It may be said, that in these cases, we correct one experience by another, but that throughout we never leave the field of experience. But the question is, how inseparable associations are formed, and Mill tells us that unless experience is invariable, no inseparable association can be formed. " Uniformities of sequence in which the phenomena succeed one another only at a certain interval, do not give rise to inseparable associations." And again, " Had but experience afforded

* Cf. Mahaffy's " Fischer on Kant." Introduction, p. xxvii.

an illusion, the counter-association formed might have been sufficient to render the reverse supposition possible." But here, experience does afford illusions, therefore inseparable associations cannot be formed. Therefore experience cannot lead up to Necessity and Universality and Inconceivability of the Opposite.

The fact is, as it seems to me, that whether we compare these rigid tests with the associations which experience generates, or whether taking experience, we see whether it is invariable enough to produce inseparable association — from both points of view, Necessary Truth remains as an unique testimony to *a priori* mental action, depending on mental forms, independent of all experience, and therefore never itself to be developed out of experience.

CHAPTER IX.

GENERAL IDEAS.

WE come now to a subject which brings us to the borderland of Logic—that of the formation of General Ideas.

Mill's view on this question is to be gathered from

(1.) Examination of Hamilton, c. xvii. "On General Concepts."

(2.) Logic. Bk. iv., c. ii., "On Abstraction, or the Formation of Conceptions."

The last chapter may be dismissed after a very few words. It is concerned only with abstraction, as a Logical process, as a process subsidary to Induction.

One pertinent criticism of Whewell may be noticed. Whewell had maintained that the conception, first formed in the mind, was superinduced upon phenomena. Mill asserts that it is only gained from phenomena. General concepts are always gained by abstraction from individual objects, whether those individual objects be the very things we are examining, or whether they be things whose resemblances we remember to have noted on former occasions, which we bring in to help out our present investigation.

The metaphysical question, how concepts are formed at all, or whether we ought to speak of General Ideas, or only of General Names, Mill does not discuss in the Logic. To discover this we have to turn to the chapter in " the Examination."

As however this question of General Ideas has a history—we had better trace its origin farther back, and let Mill's opinion, as divulged in this chapter, fall into its proper historical position, as that of a modern Nominalist.

To the Greeks, the possibility of knowledge rested in large measure on the existence of Universals or General Ideas. This was the direct outcome of, and reaction against, the Sceptical tendencies of Sophistic thought, with the stress it laid on individualism—individualism in Logic, Ethics, and Life. To Socrates the only safeguard for knowledge was the recognition of universal concepts, true for all intelligence and not varying with the variability of individuals. And so it is Socrates' praise in the mouth of Aristotle, that he insisted on the importance, not only of ἐπακτικοὶ λόγοι but also of τὸ ὁρίζεσθαι καθόλου,—that he invented a philosophy of Conceptualism. After him the artistic Hellenic feeling that for every mental idea there must be found an external counterpart, gained free play. If there are General Ideas in the mind there must be general things or Substantive Ideas in the Universe. If there are subjective ἰδέαι, arrived at by a process of comparison and division, by ξυναγωγή and διαίρεσις, there are also objective ἰδέαι, existing for Plato in the only real sense of " existence,"—in an intelligible world. Illustrated and explained in every variety of dialectical exegesis throughout all the Platonic dialogues, nowhere do the ἰδέαι stand out in such complete objective presentation as in the Republic. But not only are these universals objective and real, but they are the only reality: single, particular, individual objects fade into all the transitoriness and nothingness of the φαινόμενον. This was the extreme expression of what was known afterwards as Realism, or the doctrine of " Universalia ante rem or extra rem."

The poetry of such a conception survived in the Middle Ages, although the practical exigencies of Logic demanded its demolition at the hands of Aristotle. But Aristotle was too much of a Platonist to destroy it utterly. In his controversial moods he says, sternly enough, that such Universals were a needless reduplication of sensible things, were practically useless, and untrue; and then, in his meditative moods, he tells us, as in the Posterior Analytics, that though the individual object be the only thing perceived, yet the object of the perception is not the individual Callias, but the universal man. The only reality is affirmed to be the Hoc Aliquid, the particular sensible thing, and the Universal only the predicate of the τόδε τι: and yet all the ἀρχαὶ on which ἐπιστήμη, or Science, depends are Generals and Universals, Summa Genera, attainable only by νοῦς. The solution of the antithesis is perhaps to be found in the sentence ἐν τοῖς εἴδεσι τοῖς αἰσθητοῖς ἔνεστι πως τὰ νοητά. Νοῦς is implicit in, may be developed from αἴσθησις.* And so of Aristotle's doctrine, on this subject, the sum is that he supposed Universalia, not "extra rem" as Plato did, but "in re."

It was natural, perhaps, that Mediævalism, with its poetry, its constructive imagination, its scientific impotence, should remember the "Universalia," and forget the "in re." The doctrines of Realism,† at all events, flourished in the Schools, and Scholasticism, hand in hand with Theology, affirmed by the mouths of Anselm, Aquinas, and Duns Scotus, the existence of Universals in nature, as realities, apart from and greater than individual realities.

The reaction came in the rise of Nominalism. These Universalia were not "ante rem," or "in re," but mere "nomina," "names" applied for our convenience, holding together a mass of particulars solely by the strength of the common name applied. They are *voces*, said

---

* Arist., De An. iii.

† I need scarcely say that "Realism" in this sense is different from the sense in which I have used it as applicable to the doctrines of "Common Sense."

Roscellin. They are *sermones*, said Abelard. They are only " in mente," said William of Ockham. " Entia non multiplicanda sunt præter necessitatem." Logic, Science, the Modern Spirit were all on the side of the Nominalists, and Realism fell.

It left not itself without witness, however, in the modern world, in the doctrines of so-called Conceptualism. But, though the inheritor of Realism, the whole point of view is changed. For " Universalia" in Nature being denied and discredited, the modern question became, not whether there are or are not in Nature essences and quiddities, but rather what is the process of the acquisition of knowledge? Are these General Ideas in the Mind abstracted from particulars of Sense-perception? Or is it truer to say that, after observation of phenomena, we choose to apply not General Ideas, but merely General Names? If *a. b. c.* be observed singly and separately, is the *abc* with which we sum up the result, a general idea formed in the mind, or a general name formed, as convenience suggests, by dropping out individual peculiarities? Thus the modern contest of Conceptualism and Nominalism is waged round the origin and process of Knowledge, while the anciest contest of Realism and Nominalism was waged round the constitution of the external world. Descartes and the Cartesians are Conceptualists; Hobbes is a Nominalist; Locke is a Nominalist in tendency and a Conceptualist in expression ("words become general by being made the signs of general ideas.")* Berkeley and Hume are both claimed as Nominalists, Reid and Hamilton are, for all practical purposes, Conceptualists.

We come now, historically to the position of Mill. The chapter on "Concepts" is a criticism on Hamilton's position in this question. Hamilton, somewhat infelicitously, attempted to combine the doctrines of Conceptualism and Nominalism. He is, in reality, says Mill, a Conceptualist, yet he quotes with approbation Berkeley's words in the "Principles," in which that philosopher confesses that if others have "this wonderful power of abstracting their ideas," they best can tell, but for himself he has no such power.

There are two arguments by which Hamilton defends the possibility of General Concepts.

(i.) General Concepts are objects of the Thinking Faculty (Begriff), not objects of the Imagining Faculty (Anschauung). If we had only the Imagining Faculty we should never get beyond a series of individuals and particulars; by the aid of the Thinking Faculty we gain General Concepts. Thus though Imagination cannot figure to itself anything general or universal, Thought Proper, or the Comparative Faculty, or the Understanding, can.

This Mill denies. The distinction is one, he thinks, which would not be admitted by Berkeley, or any of

* "Essay," bk. iii. c. iii.

the great Nominalist thinkers, any more than it would be by himself.

(ii.) The second argument is that a Concept is really a mental relation between individual things. Though things be individual, the relation can be general or universal. Mill replies that a relation must mean a relation between things: and if the things are individual, so is the relation. It follows, too, that a relation cannot be thought without thinking the related objects, and the related objects being thought as individual, the relation itself is thought as individual.

After these criticisms on Hamilton, Mill states his own position, the usual Nominalist doctrine. It is this * " The formation of a Concept does not consist in separating the attributes which are said to compose it, from all other attributes of the same object, and enabling us to conceive those attributes, disjoined from any others. We neither conceive them nor think them, or cognise them in any way as a thing apart, but solely as forming the idea of an individual object." General Concepts, therefore, we have, properly, none; we have only complex ideas of objects in the concrete; we are only thinking of individual objects, but we can attend exclusively to some part of the concrete idea. And what enables us to do this is the employment of Signs and especially of Names.

There are one or two criticisms which might be

* " Examination," p. 377.

made on the way in which Mill treats Hamilton. In the first place, Mill quotes from Berkeley's "Introduction to Principles of Human Knowledge," the section 10 which is generally quoted—so far as it goes a very clear enunciation of a Nominalist position. But another section (section 15) introduces a point of view not strictly in harmony with a consistent Nominalism. "A word becomes general," Berkeley thinks, "by involving a *symbolical* relation to other things." "Universality does not consist in the absolute positive nature of anything but in the relation it bears to the particulars signified or represented by it: by virtue whereof things particular are rendered universal." It is clear then that to Berkeley "ideas" in themselves *particular* are universalised by their *relations*,—the apprehension of relations being the essence of general knowledge. If such is Berkeley's position, it is obvious that he is not a Nominalist in the sense in which Mill takes him to be. Such a position as is disclosed in the sentences given above explains, in reality, what Hamilton was aiming at, in describing General Ideas as relations.

Mill's criticism on the doctrine, which resolves General Ideas into relations, shows clearly how little he attempted to realise what Hamilton (and Berkeley before him) had meant by the word "relation." If "relation" only means a link connecting two things, it is possible that if the things are particular and individual, the link may be particular and individual also. But " relation" does not only mean "link of connection:" it means "aspects," "ways" of regarding things. "Relations established between things," means the things grasped and held together by a conception or conceptions. Relation is only another way of speaking of "mental forms." If this is the meaning which Hamilton gave (or intended to give) to the word, the criticism of Mill does not hit the point at all. However particular and individual the things may be, the view, the aspect in which they are regarded is not individual and particular. The mental form, the mould, as it were, in which the things are run, is on the contrary necessarily general and universal. Objects, as Berkeley seems to have thought, in themselves particular, are universalised by their relations.

This too explains what Hamilton meant by that "potential generality" or "universality" of certain things, of which Mill is so incredulous. It is exactly what Berkeley said when he spoke of things involving a symbolical relation to other things. All that is meant is that a triangle may be taken to stand for any and every triangle; we may reason about it, draw deductions from it, applicable to all triangles, with perfect truth. Why? Because the triangle is potentially, though not actually, universal. Because the particular triangle "doth equally stand for and represent all rectilineal triangles whatever."

And finally we see now Hamilton's distinction between Imagination and Thought—between " Anschauung" and "Begriff" in reference to this question, though, by a verbal slip, he, as Mill points out, afterwards confounds the two. A particular individual triangle is a matter for the Imaginative faculty, the Anschauung to present. It must be a triangle of some one kind, either scalene, or isosceles, or equiangular. The potential universality of that triangle, its symbolical relation to all other triangles, cannot be presented by the Imaginative faculty. It is a matter for thought, for Begriff. Or in other words, that conception of relations, which is the essence of knowledge, is the work of something higher than Sense or Imagination or any purely Presentative faculty; it is the work of Mind or Thought, imposing its own forms on the chaotic materials of Sense.

The real elucidation of the question of Conceptualism or Nominalism is not reached, until we answer the preliminary question, What is the course or progress of acquiring Knowledge? Does Knowledge proceed from the Abstract to the Concrete, or from the Concrete to the Abstract?

Locke, Hume, Mill and all Nominalists assume that the last is the true answer. First individual, concrete, objects, then abstractions from these, in so called ideas. From this point of view, of course, the ideas, being mere copies of things, cannot contain more than the things from which they are derived. There cannot, for instance, be ideas really general or universal, because this would be to add something, not accounted for by the particular, individual things of which they are the copies. Hence the Nominalist doctrine that whatever generality or universality we have or seem to have in our ideas, is a mere generality or universality of Name. Knowledge is from Concrete to Abstract, and concrete things being individual, the abstract ideas are in reality merely individual also.

Take the other assumption and the question must be differently answered. For now the assumption is that the course of knowledge is from Abstract to Concrete; that in the first stages we have vague generalities, indefinite and undefined relations, and that the development of knowledge, by Comparison, by the exercise of the Comparative or Rational faculty, leads to the increasing definiteness of these early and vague specifications until is reached the Concrete Individual Thing. For an Individual Thing, a Concrete thing, is, in reality, very complex and by no means simple, or immediately cognised. A Concrete Individual Thing has a mass of relations with other things, which keep it in its Individuality, relating it to, differentiating it from, all other things. It cannot therefore be an early product of knowledge. First there is the chaos of Sense-impressions into which the Mind brings order, by imposing forms and relations and categories. Then from the action and re-action of Sense-impressions and Thought-relation, arises the definite Individual Thing. The course of knowledge is from Abstract to Concrete.

Let us apply this to the case before us. Let us take any general Proposition. Every triangle has its three interior angles equal to two right angles. This general proposition is based, we say, on the general idea of a triangle. How has this general proposition arisen? It has arisen from a certain "analysis in reflection"* of our general idea of a triangle. Our idea of a triangle is due to "the unconscious synthesis of Perception." The Perception of a triangle is the result of certain relations being imposed on sense-impressions. These relations are imposed almost unconsciously, the normal process in perception being in all cases alike. The general proposition then is the result of an analysis in reflection of that synthesis, or imposing of relations, which goes on unconsciously in perception.

First knowledge is abstract, then it is concrete; first it is an undigested mass of general relations, then it is definite individualisation. First there is the general abstract idea of a triangle; then (and only in the second place) there is the special individual triangle whether scalene or isosceles or equiangular. When after all this process is concluded (almost unconsciously) we

* Cf. Professor Green's "Introduction to Hume," p. 183.

L

make a general proposition and enquire on what it rests, and what account we are to give of it, we answer that it is due to reflective analysis—reflection analysing the general relations imposed when knowledge was in its abstract stage.

To ask then, are General Ideas possible? is a needless question. For general ideas are of course abstract ideas: and knowledge is abstract before it becomes individual and concrete. To make General Ideas merely individual ideas, with some specific properties dropped out, is to confuse the later stages of knowledge with the earlier: to make the course of knowledge proceed from the Concrete to the Abstract, instead of (as it really does) from the Abstract to the Concrete.

If all this be so, we can see how it acts upon the Theory of Syllogistic reasoning. For the Theory of the Syllogism is really an answer to the question, what is the place of General Ideas in reasoning? Mill, consistently with his views of General Ideas, has to deny to the Major Premiss any logical merit as that from which the conclusion is proved. The conclusion does not follow from the Major Premiss, according to Mill. The Major Premiss is but a register, a memorandum of that, to which experience has testified hitherto. When we say, " All men are mortal, Socrates is a man, therefore Socrates is mortal," the conclusion does not follow from the assertion that all men are mortal, but that assertion is proved concurrently with the conclusion, by the course of experience. Mill could not say otherwise. As there are no General Ideas, knowledge must of course be a course of inference from Particular to Particular. But if there are, after all, General Ideas, as the Conceptualist imagines, it is a different thing. Then the Major Premiss becomes something more than a mere register, a memorandum. To it in a very real sense is due the conclusion. The "mortality" which we now formally predicate of man is the recognition by reflective analysis of those early relations, by which we made real and intelligible to ourselves our conceptions of humankind.

CHAPTER X.

EPILOGUE.

WITH the questions of "Necessary Truth," and "General Concepts," an inquiry into the metaphysical foundations of Mill's Philosophy necessarily ends. The special logical doctrines of Mill's "System of Logic" I have not the power or the wish to criticise. It is, in fact, part of the contention of the foregoing pages, that the logical doctrines stand on a different basis, as compared with the psychological doctrines revealed whether in criticisms of Hamilton, or expositions of James Mill. Nor is it possible for me to discuss that gravest of metaphysical questions, which forms the subject of Mill's posthumous volume on Nature and Religion. Two remarks may be ventured on. In the first place, it is not hard to discover in Mill's views as to God the result of those radical defects of Sensationalism, which are to be found in other parts of his philosophical scheme. It would be difficult, indeed, for Sensationalism, with its two dogmas of the supremacy of the Individual, and the supremacy of Sensation, to arrive at any such conceptions of the Absolute, and the Infinite, and the Super-sensual, as are implied in the philosophical (and popular) belief in the great First Cause. The attempt has twice been made by English Sensationalists, and the result has not been encouraging. In Locke,* the inconsistency of a quasi-materialism on the one side, and a proof of God, which rests on the existence of Spirit, on the other, is too obvious and apparent: and Berkeley's proof of God,† makes the conception rest on just those "presuppositions of Faith," on which, in reality, is based his doctrine of Mind or Spirit. Hume, with his clear-headed logic, and directness of vision, knew too well the limits of the sensationalistic system.

The other remark is, that Mill's view of Nature— in which the absence of all feeling of *the beauty* of the Natural World is so significant a feature—is perhaps explained by the deficiency of any systematic treatment of the Emotions, which is a peculiar characteristic of nearly all the so-called English Psychological School, with the exception of Bain. In Mill's own case, the complete subjection of his own mind in its earlier stages to that of his father (from which it comes that Mill has no Psychology of his own at all, but only an adapted version of the "Analysis" of James Mill), and the peculiar suppression of emotional culture, which his education exhibited, go far to explain these and other

---

* "Essay," b. 4, c. 3, para. 6. Cf. b. 1, c. 4, para. 8, and b. 4, c. 10.
† Cf. "Siris," and "Principles of Human Knowledge," sec. 98.

points, as well in his Philosophy, as in his Life.
"The Autobiography" should be read side by side with
the "Three Essays on Religion."*

To speak of systems of Philosophy as "transitional,"
is the easy and possibly the historical method, when
they include some curious inconsistencies. If such a
method may be employed here, Mill's system may justly
be termed "transitional." Sensationalism is the early
phase of English philosophy, Scientific Empiricism is
the later. The difference is exactly measured by the
rise and study of Biology. Sensationalism is empiricism *minus* Biology; scientific empiricism is empiricism *plus* Biology. Hume forms the apex, as it
were, of the early phase; the later phase reaches its
culmination in works like G. H. Lewes' "Problems of
Life and Mind," and the "Physical Basis of Mind."
Mill stands between the earlier and the later, he is
not a pure Sensationalist, and he is not a scientific
Empiricist. And so, if we judge him by an absolute
standard, he is doubly wrong,—wrong from the point
of view of the earlier philosophers, and wrong from the
point of view of the later. But if we view him
historically, according to a relative standard, he becomes
a true and valuable link of connection showing how
sensationalism merges itself into a scientific empiricism.
His work is, in fact, "transitional."

* Cf. Autobiography, p. 148. "I wanted a culture of the emotions."
Cf. however, p. 147.

Many indications may be found in his philosophy, which yield this result, besides some of those we have been in past pages considering. The characteristic principle of Sensationalism is the passivity of Sense, the passivity of Mind, and thence comes all the difficulty of understanding how a purely receptive and passive mind can "relate" one feeling to another, can differentiate and discriminate different sensations, can associate one with another. Biology has radically altered the problem. For now, instead of "a passive receptivity of sense," we hear of "a nervous organisation," which is active; we hear of an *organic* classification of relations, whereby the perceptions of difference and similarity are the first constituents of consciousness. "To rest with the unqualified assertion," says Herbert Spencer, "that antecedent to experience, the mind is a blank, is to ignore the questions—Whence comes the power of organising experiences?—If at birth there exists nothing but a passive receptivity of impressions, why is not a horse as educable as a man? Understood in its current form, the experience-hypothesis implies that the presence of a definitely-organised nervous system is a circumstance of no moment—a fact, not needing to be taken into account! Yet it is the all-important fact—the fact to which, in one sense, the criticisms of Leibnitz and others pointed—the fact, without which such an assimilation of experiences is inexplicable." * And Lewes, too, is equally clear on this point. He discriminates between "sensation properly so-called," and what he terms "ideation" (or the faculty of having ideas), and he pertinently asks "If the mind is 'a tabula rasa' as to knowledge, and is not even pre-existent as a faculty (according to the metaphysicians) or as organism (according to the biologists), if, in a word, sensations and combinations of sensations create both knowledge and the knowing faculties, how can we explain the phenomena of idiocy?" † Compared with this empirical development, Mill's psychological criticisms of Hamilton are somewhat antiquated. Hear him in a later work, standing before Mr. Bain's psychological labours and commenting on what to him is a new revelation. "Those who have studied the writings of the Association Psychologists, must have often been unfavourably impressed by the almost total absence, in their analytical expositions, of the recognition of any active element, as spontaneity, in the mind itself." ‡

Besides the direct contribution of Biology to Psychology in the shape of a "definitely-constituted nervous organism," there is also the indirect result of the study of Heredity. "Hereditary transmission," with all that it entails, is perhaps the most conspicuous

* H. Spencer's " Psychology," vol. i., pp. 467, 468.
† Lewes, on " Condillac," " History of Philosophy," vol. ii.
‡ Mill's " Dissertations and Discussions," vol. iii., art. on " Bain."

principle of modern scientific empiricism. It is this which explains, or is believed to explain, the long-debated question of "Mental Forms," and reconciles, as Mr. Herbert Spencer says in "First Principles," the school of Kant with the school of Locke, and allows the long-arrested development of Psychology to begin anew. For the "priority" of Forms is shown to be a mere logical priority,—the explanation being that they have been developed by a long course of experiences in the race. In other words, in these and kindred problems the great conception of Historical Evolution plays an important part. But Mill, as we have before noticed, is strangely uninfluenced by the importance of Evolution in Psychology. In this matter, he is still a Sensationalist, still clings to the individual experience of Locke and Berkeley and Hume, instead of the universal Race-experience of Herbert Spencer and Lewes. Very noteworthy, from this point of view, is his admiration of Comte's historical law of Progress; his surprise at the daring generalisation of an evolution of Thought.* In the matter of later research into "nervous organisations" and so forth, he is full of surprise and admiration at Bain; in the conception of Development, he is full of surprise and admiration at Comte. These are exactly the characteristics of a man who forms a link between two phases of a philosophical system, who connects together Sensationalism and

* In "Comte and Positivism."

Scientific Empiricism. A follower of Hume, he yet sees the imperfections of Sensationalism (as *e.g.* in the doctrine of "Causation"): a pioneer of Herbert Spencer and Lewes, he admires from a distance biological analysis, and historical evolution.

For, to those who are conversant with later speculations, it is clear that the relation between Idealism and Sensationalism is a somewhat different matter to the attitude which the metaphysician must adopt before the scientific empiricism and biology of the later school. In this particular instance of hereditary transmission of "Forms," it is of course, open to an objector to say that it only puts the difficulty a stage further back,—and that we *now* want to know how the first man who opened his eyes on the natural world proceeded to systematise his experience, whereas we took before, a man of the present time, to serve as subject for psychological analysis. But it is clear that such an answer will not be in any way satisfactory to the biologist, nor does it show much comprehension of the bearings of Evolution. For the reply that will be made will be that Intelligence is itself based, by Evolution, on Instinct, and Instinct on still lower automatic functions, and that consequently "Mental forms" were, possibly, in process of construction in much lower organisms than Man. That the metaphysician has his own unanswerable analysis of Consciousness, and Relativity of Knowledge, is, of course, undoubted; if it were proved, perfectly incontestably, that man is developed from apes, or skin-bags, it is none the less true that the consciousness which makes us men, is independent of time and development: but that the methods of Empiricism in the hands of a Lewes, are not the same as those in the hands of a Mill, is a point which, though clear enough (especially after a perusal of the imitators of Spencer), seems to have been hardly sufficiently considered. Just in the same way, Scientific Materialism has its own special views in Ethical theory,* which are by no means the same as the Ethics of Mill,—a point which is equally forgotten by those, who think that in answering utilitarianism, they are answering the moral problems of physiologists. Evolution and " a nervous organisation " play as much part in Ethics, as they do in problems of knowledge.

It is this transitional character of Mill's philosophical system which makes it, as it seems to me, so imperfect an instrument of education. For the belief is common that Mill is the modern experimental philosopher *par excellence,* that in his various works we may find the most recent and best accredited utterances of the experimental school. For this, however, we ought rather to turn to Herbert Spencer and G. H. Lewes. Mill's "Logic" is, of course,

* Cf. for instance, Maudsley; esp. "Conscience and Organisation," in " Body and Mind."

to a large extent, exempted from such criticism, but only because, to a large extent, it disavows the metaphysical foundation of the " Examination." Yet even here, in those Logical questions which depend upon metaphysical considerations,—as the question of General Ideas, and Abstraction, and possibly, too, the theory of Real Kinds in Nature,—the instability of the foundation will make itself felt. And, at all events, the student of Mill's " Logic " cannot well be debarred from the study of Mill's deeper, fundamental inquiries. For, as Mill says, with a prophetic insight, of which possibly he did not see the full application, " the difficulties of Metaphysics lie at the root of all Science."

THE END.

BRADBURY, AGNEW, & CO., PRINTERS, WHITEFRIARS.

www.ingramcontent.com/pod-product-compliance
Lightning Source LLC
Chambersburg PA
CBHW022116160426
43197CB00009B/1046